WE SWITCHED CAREERS!

Alternative Licensure Teachers' Journeys to the Classroom

EDITED BY MERVYN J. WIGHTING

FOREWORD BY C. EMILY FEISTRITZER

WATERTREE PRESS

We Switched Careers!
Alternative Licensure Teachers' Journeys to the Classroom

Copyright ©2016 by Mervyn J. Wighting

Published by Watertree Press, LLC
PO Box 16763, Chesapeake, VA 23328
http://www.watertreepress.com

Publisher's Cataloging-in-Publication Data

Names: Wighting, Mervyn J., editor
Title: We Switched Careers!
Alternative Licensure Teachers' Journeys to the Classroom
Description: Chesapeake, VA: Watertree Press LLC, 2016
Identifiers: ISBN: 978-0-9911046-8-0 (pbk.)
Subjects: LCSH: Teachers–Training of. | Teacher education. | Teachers'
    backgrounds. BISAC: EDUCATION / Training & Certification. |
    EDUCATION / Professional Development. | EDUCATION / Teaching
    Methods & Materials / General.
Classification: LCC LB1025 | DDC 371.12–dc22

Printed in the United States of America

CONTENTS

Foreword by C. Emily Feistritzer
Introduction by Mervyn J. Wighting

FOREWORD
by C. Emily Feistritzer

Dr. Feistritzer is the Founder and CEO of TEACH-NOW, an online, global alternative teacher certification program, having been President and CEO of the National Center for Alternative Certification and of the National Center for Education Information.

I T GIVES ME GREAT PLEASURE to write the foreword to this book. The alternative route to obtaining a teaching license (as opposed to a traditional four-year college program) started in New Jersey, California and Texas in the mid-1980s. All states now have an alternative route that prepares high-quality teachers. This book provides stories by 12 teachers who went through the Career Switcher program at Regent University in Virginia. Their stories are compelling and are replicated by thousands who have gone through such programs all over the country.

Alternative routes to teaching have revolutionized the profession. About 40 percent of all new teachers are now entering the profession through them. They bring an invaluable asset to the classroom – their life experiences which they can share with children at the same time as teaching them. In addition to being highly qualified teachers they are often excellent role models, and their ability to relate the curriculum to the real world that they have worked in is welcomed by school administrators.

Research indicates that alternative licensure teachers are more likely to remain in the profession than traditionally prepared colleagues, and data show that their impact on children's learning is equally as good as their colleagues. They make excellent teachers!

If you are contemplating changing careers and transitioning to teaching, I highly recommend this book to you. The stories are real, insightful and compelling. You may be able to identify with one or more of the authors, and it may very well encourage you to become a Career Switcher yourself!

INTRODUCTION
by Mervyn J. Wighting

Dr. Wighting is a Professor at Regent University in Virginia Beach and has chaired the Career Switcher program since its inception at Regent in 2004.

THIS BOOK COMPRISES THE STORIES of twelve journeys – the road traveled by former business people, members of the military, pastors, engineers and bankers all of whom responded to the calling to become a teacher. Its purpose is to inspire others who might be contemplating a similar journey in order to transition into teaching. Each of the twelve chapters tells a unique story, and the reader can rest assured that everything in each chapter is absolutely true!

Career Switchers are risk takers. In many instances they leave secure and well paid jobs in order to venture into the unknown world of education and they do this so that they can make a difference in the lives of children. They become students themselves to complete the coursework, they compete with all other candidates to get hired, and they subject themselves to the challenges of teaching instead of remaining in the comfort zone of their previous career.

Whenever I ask Career Switchers why they embarked on this journey the response is inevitably that they want to give something back. Their life experiences and their desire to help children is what they give back, and they give this unconditionally. Career Switchers bring something special into their classroom, and the whole school benefits accordingly.

The inspirational teachers you will meet in this book are responsible for educating the future generation. Each one is doing an outstanding job at this and I hope that two very precious members of the next generation will be taught by teachers who are equally good; I dedicate this book to my grandchildren Lottie and Finn.

CHAPTER ONE
Transitioning to My Third Career
by Sandy Alberson

Mr. Alberson entered the Career Switcher program in 2009 and he is currently teaching engineering courses at Landstown Governor's STEM and Technology Academy in Virginia Beach.

I GRADUATED WITH A BACHELOR'S DEGREE in Electrical Engineering and Technology in December 1975. In my senior year, enticingly near the end of the degree program, (it took me five and a half years to complete a four-year program, so please humor me!), I developed two desires to accomplish upon graduation. The first was to find a job designing computer programs or systems, digital logic circuits, etc. The second was to avoid having to take any job that required involvement with radio frequencies (R.F.), transmitters, antennas, or high voltages: items I unlovingly referred to as "fairy dust."

My fiancé, Susan, and I had chosen our wedding day, and it was now less than a year away. Believing it necessary for at least one of us to have a job before the big day, I began searching for a 'real' job. I went on several interviews but got nowhere. After much searching and interviewing (not to mention worrying), I finally found a job at Scientific Atlanta (S-A), a company known for developing satellite communications systems – radio frequencies, R.F., high voltage transmitters, "fairy dust" – aarrrgh! It was immediately obvious that everything was falling into place during the interview and since nothing else was working, I gratefully accepted the position I was offered. It was a remarkably enjoyable learning experience. Two hours each day for several weeks we had classes in the practical applications of all the subjects I had tried to avoid during college. I gradually learned to love R.F., high voltages, Atlanta's airport, lots of overtime, and the dreaded "fairy dust." It was also confirmation of the old Jewish idiom, "Man plans…God laughs."

What began as a job repairing, tuning and testing circuit boards led within weeks to a job designing, building and installing satellite uplinks and downlinks all across the country. I was actually beginning to think I had been blessed with an enjoyable job with a bright and interesting future. For the next two years I designed, tested, and installed equipment. I trained operators, and met well-known people desiring to begin the programming of a channel that we now know as cable television. I even learned how to navigate the rules and regulations of the Federal Communications Commission.

One of the satellite uplinks purchased from S-A went to the Christian Broadcasting Network (CBN), headed by Pat Robertson. I'd often thought mass domestic and international communications would be a natural for ministries and now it looked like that was coming to pass – and I might just get to be a part of it. Dr. Robertson turned out to be a fascinating person, able to speak intelligently about both Biblical Exegesis and klystron R.F. amplifiers all in the same conversation!

Shortly after we'd completed the installation, CBN's Director of Engineering asked if I would consider coming on staff to manage the facility. This was an exciting offer as far as I was concerned and after consulting with my wife and a great deal of conversation with fellow engineers, I accepted the position of CBN's Manager of Satellite Communications. In that position I worked with radio and television affiliates, plus cable television companies who carried the "CBN Cable Network" that was later known as the "Family Channel." I was with CBN's engineering department from its inception in 1978 until the Family Channel was sold in 1997.

My wife and I began preparing for the inevitable change as soon as it became clear that the Family Channel was to be sold. Shortly after the sale, my once very busy job at CBN become extremely mundane and frustratingly boring. Telling no one outside my family, I decided to resign from CBN and simply wait to see what openings presented themselves for employment. My last day at CBN was on a Friday and on the following Sunday I was asked to consider becoming the Director of Communications at our church. This held much interest for me as I could build on what I already knew technologically, and be challenged by the many aspects of the job I couldn't yet imagine. I agreed to accept the new position.

Two years later, I was informed by the new senior pastor that in order to continue to work as now a senior staff member I would be need to be ordained as a minister and I would require a master's degree from one of our seminaries. The only alternative was to be released from my church position. The thought of learning more theology was very appealing and I looked forward to attaining a Master's degree. Going back to school part-time, it took me seven and a half years to finish all the requirements to obtain my degree in Christian Education. I enjoyed every class of every course I took. My diploma read "Master of Arts in Christian Education" from Southeastern Baptist Theological Seminary. The date was December 14, 2007 and I graduated just in time to see the economy nose dive, donations at the church to decline, and the need for reductions in staff. After being on the church staff for ten years I was informed in October 2008 that I needed to find other employment no later than the next April. For almost six months my wife and I had both experienced a feeling that things weren't going well and that another change was forthcoming. It was time yet again for us to look at my options, determine if I needed and could afford any additional education to further my career, and possibly to make another major change in direction.

One night several weeks after being told of my forthcoming layoff, my wife asked me what I wanted to do. "Something enjoyable that won't require all the travel that had been required in the past" was all I could think to say. Susan and I had co-taught a young adults class at church for several years, and in my first career I'd taught engineers and technicians the technicalities and legalities of satellite communications. On Susan's advice, I took a personality profile and personal gifts test that showed my number one personality trait was enjoying being around people and that my number one gift was teaching. Right then I began to think seriously about becoming a public or private school math or science teacher. The idea was intriguing enough to explore the possibility further and I began preliminary research on the requirements needed to obtain a license in order to teach middle or high school students.

My wife and I had both noticed that morning television commercials were replete with advertisements indicating a local school system was partnering to help prepare Career Switchers for the classroom. Two local universities were advertising Career Switcher programs: Old Dominion University and Regent University. I investigated both, and found Regent's program much more to my liking. Regent appeared to have an excellent program with alumni who were well respected by other teachers I knew. I was told that Regent's professors were consistently interested in and supportive of their students and, very importantly, Regent was miles closer to our home!

My previous experiences with CBN had required some minor involvement with Regent's professors, and I also knew several Regent staff members through our previous church. Significantly, during a conversation with an ODU professor, he told me that he thought Regent would be a better choice for me. So, I began the application process in late October and completed all of Regent's requirements just two days before the application window ended for the program beginning the following January.

One of the requirements for admission to the Career Switcher program was that applicants had to pass the Virginia Communication and Literacy Act test, and at least one Praxis II assessment before the classes began. While the VCLA wasn't a source of anxiety, I'd heard horror stories about how hard some Praxis test could be. Not being sure I could pass a Praxis exam for a high school math or sciences course on the first attempt, I choose an easier route and took two middle school exams. I was amazed at how well I did on both tests, and this increased my confidence that I might just be able to become a teacher after all!

My last day at the church was on a Thursday in January. I attended an orientation class at Regent that night and began classes the following evening. My mother often said that God's timing is never early, but never late, was ringing in my ears as I looked back on everything that had occurred in such a short period.

The Career Switcher classes were as close to perfection as I could imagine a Master's and doctoral program class structure could be. The classes, instructors, guest lecturers, curriculum, classmates, school administrators, etc. were all wonderful in my humble opinion! Many of the classes were hard, some extremely hard, even for those with years of teaching experience who were taking the some of the same classes for a 'Master Teacher' certification. Unknown to me at the time, the professors purposely let us struggle sometimes so that we would find out what we were made of, and more importantly, what we were capable of accomplishing. The more classes I attended and the more projects we completed collaboratively, the more my confidence increased. I began looking forward to my practicum work in schools, the one-year provisional license, and after that my first full five-year teaching license. My third career looked like it might be enjoyable as the first two - possibly more so – but first I had to get hired!

In late February, just seven weeks after beginning my classes at Regent, my program advisor announced to the class that a long-term substitute teaching assignment in high school sciences was available at a small Christian school in the area. I asked her if she thought I was ready for such a position. Her reply was simple, "if they don't think you will be a good fit, they will say they want to look at other candidates before making a decision." I have a tendency to not perform very well in interviews due to nervousness but thought at a minimum that I would gain additional experience in the interview process – something I hadn't subjected myself to in over a decade. To my surprise, however, the interview was actually enjoyable! My church staff background gave me a large advantage in working with people of all ages – the interviewers were looking for someone who could bridge a gap between the school board, the school staff and the school's students and parents. Surprisingly to me, I was asked to begin teaching the high school sciences – all of the high school sciences - the following week! "Be careful of what you wish for as you may just get it!" I went home with a stack of high school teacher edition textbooks several feet thick, and a case of butterflies in my stomach. Oh my gosh, what was I thinking?!

I found I could remember enough of my high school and bachelor's course materials (with the help of the full-time teacher's texts) to start teaching Earth Science, Biology, Chemistry, Physics, and Physical Science. One of the Master Teacher candidates in the university program once told me that, "sometimes you have to fake it until you can make it," and I will never know if the students understood how nervous I was in those early classes. Occasionally my knees were almost shaking, not quite – but close. It was a relief when two of my students later told me that I made their knees shake as well. "You're a good teacher. We learn and laugh during most of your classes. We understand the material but your tests are hard. You make us think!"

Within two months, I was over my nervousness, and by the end of the school year, I was hooked. At the end of the school year, I was voted 'Rookie

Teacher of the Year' at the school and was asked to come back as a full time high school science teacher the following fall. After months without a salary, the paychecks were also a welcome relief as well. Later that June, I was granted a Virginia state provisional teacher's license.

The Career Switcher program lasted two years. The first year, Regent's classes were held Thursday and Friday nights and most of the day on Saturdays. Guest lecturers were very common – and very good. My favorite adjunct professor was a practicing schoolteacher; let's call her Samantha. She was, beyond a doubt, the most gifted teacher I've ever encountered. She once had a conversation in class among seven international students and a teacher with herself playing all the parts, each with different voices and accents. To this day when I'm in doubt on how to approach a situation, I find myself asking, "What would Samantha do?"

The classes were extremely informative, challenging, and thoroughly enjoyable. We were given excellent background material, practical applications and later in the program, challenging problems to solve that teachers might confront. Classroom situations, student disagreements, personality conflicts among teachers, disagreements between teachers and the administration, problems between school and governing board, irate parents... all of these became solvable and no longer insurmountable obstacles. The projects and problems were based on the types of experiences we would face in real life. Regardless of the school, regardless of what you teach, regardless of the size of your classes, you'll face them if you enter teaching – and with a high degree of confidence if you have completed the Career Switcher program!

Instead of written exams of the type usually associated with degree level programs, our assessments were individual and group projects. Each project was tailored to expose us to aspects of the education business that we may be exposed to in our new careers. It's called 'Problem Based Learning' and is a great tool to have in your teacher's tool box. Many of these problem situations were mentally challenging but highly rewarding and built confidence when the solutions worked well. It was highly gratifying later to come across a problem while teaching that matched what you had been exposed to during the program.

Our final group project, the summative assessment, was the design of a new charter school for 'doubly exceptional' students – above average intelligence and with learning difficulties. We had to defend the school's existence against a board of directors that consisted of several of our professors, teachers who had graduated from the program previously, and the Dean of the School of Education. Our group was only the second in the program to pass the project with a perfect score!

The university's classes had prepared me wonderfully. The course materials I taught at school those first years both supplemented and validated what I had been taught in the program. Many of my fellow Regent students were seasoned teachers, studying for an advanced qualification. They were often as helpful as the instructors in assisting us newly entered Career Switchers to overcome the many things we would face: selecting curriculum appropriate to the age of the class; developing workable and interesting lesson plans; finding extra-curricular supplemental materials; test writing; student discipline issues; parent communications; getting along with other teachers and a host of other functions that teachers perform routinely.

As I began my first year in the small Christian school as an officially licensed teacher, I was asked if I would consider being the middle and high school assistant principal. How amazing!! Years earlier, I'd made a promise I never tell God, "no," to an opportunity if it looked like He was working in the situation. Based on this, I reluctantly agreed to become the 'AP'. After all, I mean really, how hard could it be in such a small school (230 students in grades three through 12)? Unbeknown to me at the time, however, a managerial problem between the school board and the administration had just erupted during the summer. It became much worse in November. In early December, the remaining administration departed and I was asked to become the middle and high school principal – while still remaining the high school science teacher! The apostle Paul is quoted as saying, "I can do all things through Christ who strengthens me." These words were ringing in my ears as I belatedly agreed to the board's request. Once again, "Man plans, God laughs." I think God must have a great sense of humor!

So what advice can I offer to those who might be about to teach? First and foremost I believe that planning is the most critical thing a teacher does. You have to look at several different time frames simultaneously. These include: 1) getting through the required material in the allotted time, 2) developing weekly lesson plans, 3) modifying those lesson plans almost daily based on how well things went previously, 4) making sure you have sufficient grades in "the system" for progress reports, report cards, etc., and 5) attempting to finish sections of the curriculum to coincide with the various school holidays. All the while, you have to develop methods of delivering curriculum while maintaining students' interest – even when you know they have an innate phobia of the material! When I was a kid, my neighbor had a talking doll. Pulling her back string made her say, "Eeeeh, I don't like math…it's too hard." Art really does imitate life sometimes. You have to change that perception for students to something more like, "I'm not going to let a word problem beat me. I eat math problems for breakfast."

Most teachers have an 'introduction speech' they give to all students during the first week of school. I always tell the students that my job isn't to just give them grades but to give them facts, mastery, and wisdom in the subject at hand. I also tell them I have two firm rules in class. The first rule is, "There is no such thing as a 'stupid' question." If they don't understand – ask. If they don't understand a point, there is a good probability that others don't either but are reluctant to ask." This first rule tends to put them at ease. The second rule is that, "They will have to fight me to fail a course." This lets them know I'm on their side – and I truly am. Science classes (and now engineering courses) tend to scare students. At a minimum, the course material makes them apprehensive. Reduce the apprehension and learning is easier – and so is teaching. To quote Financial Peace University's Dave Ramsey: "I try to put the cookies on the bottom shelf so everyone can grab them." Make things easy to understand, especially at first. You can't build a tall "wall of wisdom" if you have a weak or non-existing foundation of understanding.

At the first appropriate opportunity each year and in each class, I ask students, "How do you eat an elephant? I receive a lot of blank stares, or even worse, the "Mr. A has lost his marbles," look. The correct answer is, "Lots of small bites over a period of time." Students most readily grasp new and foreign concepts the same way, learn one small part of the solution at a time over and over until you master the entire concept. You have to convince students they can learn complex math and science concepts. Confidence builds confidence. Learning is fun for students when the "ah-ha" moments come often enough. How do you tackle a hard course? You learn one precept at a time and then build upon them throughout the year. If you can get the students to understand this and get them to become aggressive in their approach to the material they tend to do well.

Good teachers learn to read their student's facial expressions and eye movements. When I see fear or apprehension in their eyes, I ask them again, "How do you eat an elephant?" They reply, "One bite at a time." It reminds them they've been in a similar situation before and not just survived, but thrived. It also breaks the tension they feel and it lightens their mood. On the opposite side of the coin, one of the neatest things about teaching is the "Ah-ha!" moment when a student grasps a concept for the first time. The best teachers live for this! It makes all the work and all the long hours worthwhile.

My students don't all make grade A but I have had to give very few failing grades. I'm an analysis nut myself and I like to see how my students (and therefore my teaching ability) stacks up against the national averages on standardized achievement tests. I'm delighted to say they typically average 3-15 points above the mid-line when compared to the national averages on a subject by subject basis. Maybe not Rhodes Scholar material, but not bad on average.

After six years of private school salary (low!), some administrative uncertainty, and several health issues, I decided to change schools – primarily due to the financial and health concerns. I now teach in a public school in Virginia Beach at a Governor's STEM school where I am responsible for engineering and pre-engineering courses. The staff, from the principal to my fellow STEM teachers, are all wonderful. The atmosphere is great and I believe I'm helping to make a difference in the lives of students each day. What I tell my students who are looking for their first jobs applies to aspiring teachers as well: if you are prepared educationally, mentally, and socially for a position before you know it exists you can more easily walk through an open door of opportunity when it presents itself. I also tell them the same thing my favorite teacher told me – 80% of succeeding in any job is getting along with co-workers and superiors by honing your people skills.

The courses I teach are not governed by Virginia's Standards of Learning (SOL) tests. Instead of SOL's, we are governed by Virginia's CTE (Career and Technical Education), VERSO (Virginia's Educational Resource System Online) standards, and industry certification testing. The STEM school seeks to prepare students for technical and scientific pursuits. This includes engineering universities. My goal is to cover every aspect of the material as listed in the VERSO guidelines. I supplement this by contacting professors at well-known universities that offer related subjects and asking them what they would like to have their students know when they first enter their programs. I make sure my students are aware of this, and I have found this approach has many benefits. My students know I am going the extra mile for them, and it also gives me great contacts and inroads to universities all over America in related fields of interest. It lets me know what areas of the curriculum I need to concentrate on. Finally, it gives the students the knowledge that they are being prepared properly for the universities and programs in which they are interested.

Teaching is, as the saying goes, 'not just a career, it's an adventure.' The salary in public school systems is good, especially when you consider the fact that you get long vacations. The hours required in a typical week are compatible with my other careers. If you set your standards of performance and classroom policies in advance the students will meet them. In any school there will be students who will soar academically, and those who will struggle. Some of their home lives are so horrible as to defy imagination. One of the many things that makes teaching so rewarding is when a former student comes back to see you and tells you how thankful they are for your class – immediately before asking you if you can help them with a class assignment they are having problems with! It is also gratifying when a student shows you their notes from a class you taught several years earlier that they are still using. As a teacher, you really do have a part in the future of our country.

If I had to give current teachers and prospective teacher a few pieces of advice, I'd ask them to consider the following. First, you can't teach effectively what you don't understand completely -- so learn the material thoroughly before you attempt to teach it. Students will ask some off the wall questions! That is great as it means they are attempting to grasp the material and just maybe they are already trying to synthesize new uses for the information you are giving them. But equally they will quickly discover whether or not you know the material! Second, remember that there are two types of respect – positional respect and relational respect. The students may respect you at first just because you are their teacher, but that can wear off really quickly. It is far better to develop relationships with each student. The old adage that they won't care what you know until they know you care is so very true. Third, it is always better to make an ally of a student's parents or guardian before you 'need' to talk to them about their child. The best educators are team players and it is much better to have the parents on your team versus having them play for the opposition. Finally, watch your students' faces constantly, their faces are the windows to their minds. Do they understand? Are you holding their attention? Do you need to try a different tack with a lesson? Their eyes and facial expressions will tell you the answer to those all-important questions! Recently, I received a graduation invitation from a student who graduated earlier from my previous school. She had just completed her bachelor's degree at Georgetown University. I had taught a personal finance course to her class covering interest rates on loans and the hidden dangers associated with their abuse and she was applying for her first car loan when suddenly she grasped the concept of compound interest rates. I would have loved to have been a 'fly on the wall' in the finance office of the car dealer when her Aha moment occurred and, as she put it, she began giggling at how proud I would have been to hear her asking for a lower interest rate on the loan. Things like that make teaching so worthwhile, no matter what subject you may teach!

CHAPTER TWO

Memories of a Military Spouse
by Cheryl Beauchamp

Mrs. Beauchamp entered the Career Switcher program in 2011 and her most recent position was teaching STEM subjects (Advanced Placement Computer Science and Engineering 1, 2 & 3) at Coronado High School in Coronado, CA.

REMEMBER THE MAGIC 8 BALL? My children came across my old one while we were cleaning out and organizing some boxes before yet another of our Navy moves. I smiled while explaining what it was and how it worked. The Magic 8 Ball has 20 responses to questions that are asked. Ten responses are positive (It is certain; It is decidedly so; Without a doubt; Yes definitely; You may rely on it; As I see it, yes; Most likely; Outlook good; Yes; Signs point to yes). Five are negative (Don't count on it; My reply is no; My sources say no; Outlook not so good; Very doubtful), and five are neutral (Reply hazy try again; Ask again later; Better not tell you now; Cannot predict now; Concentrate and ask again). What I didn't share with them was how often I used it in high school and college while attempting to determine what path I should take in life. My friends and I would sit around during one of our high school sleep-overs and ask the Magic 8 Ball questions that included where should we live, who should we date, and what should we do after we graduated from high school. Common Magic 8 Ball responses included 'Reply hazy try again' and 'Better not tell you now'!

I didn't need to ask it if I should go to college. 'It is certain'; 'Without a doubt'; 'It is decidedly so'. I was the first one in my family on both sides to go to college. With my class ranking in the top 10% and aptitude in math and science, it was obvious to my parents and counselors that I should continue my studies in those areas. My college friends and I, while enjoying pizza in our dorm room, would again consult the Magic 8 Ball. Some asked if they should accept their boyfriend's proposal, or if they should break up with their boyfriend, some asked if they should change their major, or if they should continue to graduate school. We knew the Magic 8 Ball wouldn't really provide the true answers for us, but we enjoyed sharing our concerns with each other.

I graduated with a dual major in physics and computer science and a minor in mathematics. Two years later, I earned my Master's of Science in computer science and married my long distance boyfriend of four years. I had forgotten about the Magic 8 Ball while in graduate school. Life's path seemed pretty certain during those two years. I had a full-time job, I was going to school in the evenings, and I was in a long distance relationship with my boyfriend who was forward deployed as a U.S. Naval Officer. When I look back on that time in my life, I recall the considerations I had to make regarding my career path. Should I stay in school and complete a residency at George Washington University to become a Medical Physicist? Should I move across the continent to Silicon Valley and seek a position as a software developer? Or should I accept a marriage proposal and follow my future husband to his next duty station. My heart provided the answer for me.

Military relocations every 18 to 24 months with my husband, to places that include Monterey, CA, Norfolk, VA, and Newport, RI, provided different experiences as a software programmer. I developed software solutions for military contracting firms, a financial service company, and an online newspaper company. I enjoyed the challenges of my work, sought opportunities to learn more, and took on further responsibilities. Software engineering was a good fit for me as I enjoyed the process of coding. Coding was similar to puzzle solving: applying a strategy, testing to see if it worked, and then trying again. I enjoyed solving puzzles and when I transitioned to become technical project manager I felt this too, was a good fit. The process of managing resources to meet the constraints and criteria of a release was just another kind of puzzle solving.

Nonetheless, these positions were never more than a job, a well-paying job, but still just a job. There is some sense of job satisfaction when completing a project release successfully or when a client shares positive feedback; however, I would never say I was called to be a programmer or a project manager. I never felt this job was how I was meant to make a difference in the world.

Nonetheless, I was being paid well, I enjoyed my work environment, and I was good at what I did. I didn't plan to re-evaluate my career path. However, I was having a difficult pregnancy with my third child. I suffered from severe hyperemesis gravidarum and had already miscarried earlier in the year. I was not going to risk losing this baby; I resigned and on my last day ended up in the emergency room at the hospital. My two-day stay in the hospital as well as the bed rest I was put on at the 14 week stage provided time for my husband and me to reflect and to evaluate my choices. We decided to adjust our lives to enable me to stay home with our children. My third child was born weighing in at over nine and a half pounds, and two years later I gave birth to another very healthy ten-pound baby!

Life was very full with four children and I committed myself to being a full-time mom. However, there were always moments of questioning, especially at social engagements. Small chat introductions were about what you did for a living. Being a stay-at-home mom wasn't one that encouraged further conversations with working women. Stay-at-home moms would find each other and share tips for child rearing. Still I questioned my choices: could I again manage working while also raising my blessings?

Although I enjoyed my previous profession, I didn't want to take time away from my children. My husband and I had committed to a lifestyle that enabled me to stay home with the children. I have to admit, supporting a family of six on one income was very challenging; however, my husband and I agreed I made a difference at home much more than I did so at my previous job. I was making a difference in the lives of four young children each and every day. Still, there was a small voice that quietly asked if and when I return to working outside the home, what would I choose to do -- and I didn't have a clue.

The answer didn't come to me by consulting the Magic 8 Ball. Instead, it came through a bucket of LEGO bricks. After school clubs and sports always required at least two or three of my children to have to wait for their sibling to finish an activity before we headed home. The most effective way for keeping them entertained was by bringing along a blanket and bucket of building toys. It wasn't long before several other children were also asking to join and play with my children. Soon, I was proposing an after school enrichment program which utilized building toys to teach students about science, technology, engineering, and math. After receiving administrative approval, the club reached maximum participation with waiting lists. The program expanded to 3 days after school and there were still children on the waiting list. This was a tremendous opportunity to teach children about science and math while they were playing with LEGO bricks and other building toys. It did not seem like work; it felt more like play.

In 2010 we relocated from San Diego, California to Norfolk, Virginia due to my husband's career, however, I always found schools that were interested in my after school enrichment program. Eventually, I was asked to fill an instructor position at a school when the middle school math and science teacher resigned. Although I felt comfortable teaching basic physic concepts and math while incorporating the engineering process with the after school program, the thought of becoming an actual teacher was intimidating. I didn't have any formal education on curriculum development, classroom management, or child psychology. At the same time, I was excited. I enjoyed working with the children during the after school program and observing them embrace math and science concepts while building and testing. This was far more rewarding than any positive client feedback I received when I was a project manager. Some of these kids were considered to be the more disruptive ones in their classes and I even received advice from some teachers who felt I should not include certain students who "might be too difficult for me to manage". I was thrilled that these 'disruptive' students thrived in our after school program and were no trouble at all!

My husband and I talked at length regarding the commitment this position would require, the time it would take away from the family, and we shared the decision with our children. Unlike my previous career in which the hours required my children to be in daycare, working as a teacher would enable me to have the same hours they did. Additionally, since we shared the same holidays, I did not need a daycare solution for winter, spring, and summer breaks. My family was supportive and encouraged me to take this next step. The career switch wasn't a true change for me as it might have been if I had made the decision six years earlier when I resigned from my project management position. It was more of a step forward in the path I was already traveling. Staying at home teaching my children was the first few steps, the next step was the after school STEM enrichment program, and now the newest steps were those that would enable me to become a teacher.

I firmly believe that knowing the content that will be taught is not enough to be able to teach it to another person successfully. I observed this over and over while teaching my own children. We know how to cut with scissors or how to tie our shoes, however, teaching both of these skills to a new learner can be challenging. Proper teacher preparation was imperative if I was to become a successful educator; therefore, I applied and was accepted to Regent University's Career Switcher program. I was able to build on what I had learned previously, and the courses I took immediately impacted my ability to teach my students. I was able to implement positive classroom management practices, incorporate alternative assessments, and create action plans to engage my students and teach them more effectively. These were tools I specifically learned from the courses I took in the Career Switcher program and they made the difference in that I felt more confident that I could teach and that my students would learn. The understandings gained helped identify the student who constantly blurted out in class, repeating everything I said while I was providing direct instruction, as not being disrespectful but in fact, attempting to process the information he was hearing by repeating it vocally. It was his effective learning strategy. I gained understandings that I needed to adapt my teaching strategies to meet the needs of different learners so that the student who achieved high marks on vocabulary assessments shouldn't receive a zero because he didn't make the vocabulary index cards, since my goal is for learning the vocabulary words and not on how to make vocab index cards. I also learned there are many different types of teachers and we may have many different strategies for teaching. My instructors taught me that we should be united in our goal of educating our students instead of tearing each other down with criticism when our methods are different.

Although I have completed my formal education and earned my certification to teach, I am still a learner. I continue to enroll in education courses, attend development workshops and conferences, and meet with practicing professionals. I am constantly learning something new and find it rewarding to utilize a learned technique to reach another student and see them have their 'Aha!' moment.

I am often asked, "Why do you teach when you could return to your previous career and make a great deal more money?" I am hearing the same comments that I heard when I was in high school, "You are capable of so much more, why settle on teaching?" To be perfectly honest, the first year of teaching was very challenging. The hours are long and the work never seems finished. Others have remarked they feel our days are much shorter than their workdays as we only teach from 8:00am until 3:00pm. However, what they don't observe or recognize is that we may need to be in school at 7:00 a.m. to prepare our materials for the day, to tutor students who need the additional help, or to attend a faculty meeting. They don't see that we stay until 5:00pm or later to facilitate an after-school club or enrichment program to provide students the opportunity to further their learning in specific area of interests. They don't see the hours we spend at home grading papers, differentiating lesson plans to meet the needs of different learners, and researching alternative methods for teaching the curriculum. Comparing my previous career hours with my teaching hours, I easily put in much more time as an educator. However, it's worth it and much more fulfilling. Although exhausting, it's exciting and invigorating knowing the efforts made will impact at least one student.

During my first year of teaching middle school science I showed a video from the website water.org regarding efforts to bring clean water to the people of Uganda. We were learning about environmental science and discussing the use of plastic disposable water bottles versus tap water. Midway through our unit some of my students came to me with a campaign they were hoping to initiate at the school. They wanted to see how many students would be willing to give up using plastic disposable water bottles and drink tap water from a reusable bottle instead. Their plan was to ask people to donate the money they would have used to buy bottled water to fund a drive they were doing to raise money in order to send to water.org to build another well. These students came to me with the idea. I did not assign them this initiative. My 6th grade students wanted to make a difference and help others halfway across the globe! My students were also logging weather data on spreadsheets that were shared with students in Australia, South America, and Europe who were also logging their data on the same spreadsheets so that they could all compare their local weather with each other. My students were watering an avocado tree that was over 2 feet tall because they wondered if they planted the avocado seed it would actually grow. These are just some examples of events that occur where I get to spend my working day. There are countless more. Every week I have students that challenge me to engage them effectively. But each and every day I have students who remind me that what I am doing is worthwhile and impactful. I have found a place where I can truly make a difference.

I am a science, math, engineering, and computer science teacher. I have had the opportunity to teach students who are in elementary, middle, and high school. Additionally, I have also taught higher education STEM workshops. I believe it is imperative that we encourage our students to not only learn, but also to love learning by supporting and engaging them. I not only want to share my passion for the subjects I teach, but I also want to provide students with the skills and tools to always pursue more knowledge in these areas. My role is to help lead them not manage them; to inspire them not mold them. I am grateful I have listened and answered my calling to become a teacher. I am grateful each and every day I enter my classrooms for the opportunity to interact with students. We are partners in this learning journey.

My family is preparing for yet another Navy tour location change. We are sad to say goodbye to friends we have made during this two-year stay as we are getting ready to meet new friends at the next location we will call home. I will miss my students and hate having to say goodbye to them. Some of them will ask what my plans will be when I move. Will I teach high school again? Or will I return to teaching in a middle school? Or would I seek a higher education position at the local community college? Perhaps the Magic 8 Ball would provide some insight. Regardless of the possible responses, I do not need to ask the ball if I should continue teaching and if I should look into the requirements to do so at our next Navy duty station? 'As I see it, yes'; 'You may rely on it'; and 'Yes, definitely'!

CHAPTER THREE

A Thousand Jobs, One Career
by LaTonia Bougouneau

Ms. Bougouneau entered the Career Switcher program in 2005 and she is currently teaching English at Cradock Middle School in Portsmouth.

ON SATURDAY, NOVEMBER 27, 2004, I stood in the middle of my apartment looking at a multitude of boxes that lined the walls as they stood like soldiers on my living room floor. I did not have the official date yet, but I knew I was going to be evicted. As I moved around, I stopped in my dining area when a small booklet caught my eye. I opened the booklet and on that very page was the scripture Deuteronomy 30:11-14 in the King James Bible. It read

> For this commandment I give to you this day, it
> is not hidden from thee, neither is it far off. It is not in
> heaven, that thou shouldest say, who shall go up for us to
> heaven, and bring it unto us, that we may hear it, and do
> it? Neither is it beyond the sea, that thou shouldest say,
> who shall go over the sea for us, that we may hear it and do
> it? But the word is very nigh unto thee, in thy mouth
> and in thy heart, that thou mayest do it.

At the end of the scripture, the writer asked the question, "What did God tell you to do?" I said aloud, "Lord I did everything you told me to do…what have I not done? An hour or so later I went out for a cup of coffee and a newspaper. On the front page of the Virginian Pilot, was an article about the Career Switcher program at Old Dominion University. The article featured a teacher standing in her classroom in front of her chalkboard. I chuckled to myself and said, "Okay God". It was the beginning of my teaching career.

For ten years I served in in the United States Navy as a Hospital Corpsman and subsequently in the reserves for four years. I went into the military a few months after graduating high school. Unlike some of my classmates, I did not come from a wealthy background so my choices were limited. Upon graduating from high school, I knew three things to be true. First, I was not smart enough to get into college. Second, my grandparents could not afford to pay college tuition, and third, if I stayed in Brunswick, GA I might well become a teenage mother. So in 1987, following my high school graduation, I entered the United States Navy as a Hospital Corpsman. My goal was not to advance in a military career, but to build the finances I would need to obtain a degree in business administration so I could eventually own my own hair salon.

As a Hospital Corpsman, I worked in military clinics, hospitals, and in clinical offices. I took vital signs, drew blood, and administered immunizations. I pulled twelve-hour shifts on the labor and delivery ward instructing mothers on how to nurse and care for their newborns. I coordinated medical evacuations for patients overseas in need of specialized treatment in the United States and abroad. I held certifications as an EMT, CPR instructor, HIV/AIDS Instructor, and as a mail handler. You name it, I did it! Because I never intended to stay in the military, I allowed time to pass without advancing in a timely manner and that led to my leaving at the ten-year mark. I never intended to stay longer than four years, but as the old adage goes, I failed to plan and thus, my plan failed. With a failing marriage and the birth of my second child, I was forced to leave the military. With all of my experience and with a laundry list of credentials that were valid in the private sector, I was offered a mere $7.30 an hour for my first civilian job.

With my severance money from the military I purchased a new home, a new car, and added to that total a $700.00 per month daycare bill. In less than three months of my discharge from the military, I was in bankruptcy court. I worked as a lead cashier at Target and I joined the Navy reserves. It just was not enough. Three years later I was divorced and barely making it. Enough was enough. One day I looked at my paystub and it read $9.30 an hour and I told my supervisor to take me off the schedule because I had decided I was going back to school full time.

Fast forward three years and I graduated from Norfolk State University in 2002 with a B.A. in Journalism. I then took a gamble and instead of continuing my education, I attempted to enter the workforce, but to my dismay, I was only able to find temporary work. To paint you a picture of my desperation to provide for my family, my list of jobs included working as a temporary benefits administrator, a temporary bankruptcy secretary, and a contracted position as an anesthesia technician, a cashier at BJ's Wholesale, the Tidewater Community College Bookstore, Wal-Mart, Macy's and Target. I worked wherever I could for as long as I could, but each job led nowhere. Eventually I was out of work again, but this time I had no prospects and life was looking grim to say the least.

I collected unemployment but that was not enough to pay the electricity bill and the water bill at the same time. Every night I feared that my vehicle would be repossessed. I could not afford make the payments and the insurance at the same time. I received child support, but still I did not have enough for everything. In a nutshell, I was laid off from my latest job as an anesthesia technician at Portsmouth Naval Hospital, my rent was behind, and my cupboards were bare. I had no more fight left. I threw my hands up and said, "Lord, I'm done, they can put me out - I quit!"

Two days following the newspaper article where I read about the Career Switcher program, I began to place calls to as many colleges as possible. I did not need another job - I needed a career! On Monday, November 29, 2004, I called Regent University to inquire about their Master's degree programs. I was looking for a program that would lead to a professional certification. The voice on the other end of the phone asked questions about what I wanted to do and he gave me an insight on what was available. I was concerned about my qualifications and my educational background. I had a bachelor's degree in journalism, so when he mentioned teaching I quickly proclaimed my lack of qualifications. "You don't need GRE scores or Praxis scores…you will have time to get that done. Do you have your unofficial transcripts?" I had everything he asked for. "Can you come to the school with these documents by 3:00 p.m. today?" "Sure" I said. His words were like music in my ears.

I arrived at the university and submitted my documents; I interviewed, and I answered a host of questions. As I sat in the waiting area I noticed papers in files that lined the walls. Among the papers a purple colored sheet stood out titled Regent Village Family Housing. As I read about the on-campus family housing, I thought to myself, what kind of school is this that will allow you and your children to live on campus. Without hesitation, I phoned to have my name placed on the waiting list. I had yet to be accepted, but in my spirit, I knew I was going to attend Regent University! In my 78-cent spiral notebook I began to shape my future. Without dates, I wrote 'sign contract, pick up keys for my new apartment, and start school'. When I signed up to rent an apartment, I was number 100 and something. I did not care. I prayed and told God this was where I wanted to live.

A few weeks later I was brought back to reality. There was the eviction notice plastered on my apartment door. Yet while material things were falling apart I was able to glean small pieces of hope from what was starting to work. I went to court over my unpaid rent and I was not spared - we had to get out. In the midst of what some would call a tragedy, however, I could see God working out the plan He had for my life. In the latter part of December I got my acceptance letter to join Regent University's Career Switcher Program in January. The night before my first day of class, my friends, my girls, and I moved furniture, boxes, and toys until 3:00 in the morning because we had until 9:00 am the next morning to vacate the premises. As we packed up the last of our things I put on a brave face for my girls. The truth was I did not know where we were going, but one thing for sure was that I had a seat in that class and that was all that mattered. As I drove away, I looked back and said "I don't know where we are going, but we are going!"

I started my first day of class just a few hours later. I sat amongst my peers full of excitement and joy all bundled up on the inside of me. No one knew my name or my story. I kept saying to myself, what a privilege it is to be here. My girls and I were able to stay at a friend's house while she was away on military leave. During my first week of school, I reached out to the manager of Regent's housing office by sending her an e-mail explaining that I was in school but I did not have a permanent residence. With a quick response, the manager informed me that there were not any apartments currently available, and added: "but we would believe God for something to become available". Two nights later, I got a phone call that I would have an apartment within the next two weeks!

The Career Switcher Program was my fast track to becoming a teacher. The joy of the Career Switcher Program for me was the short amount of time that it took to complete the courses, it led to licensure, and you could substitute teach while learning to become a teacher.

An added benefit for me was the security of having a place to live. I do not know which part of my journey was the hardest, being evicted or learning to become a teacher. Have you ever sat in class and wondered what in the world she or he (the instructor) is talking about? Well, I have because that is what I experienced during the first few weeks in the program. I passed my courses, but I would be fibbing if I said it was not a struggle.

Coming from the military and with a medical background, the world of education was new to me. I knew health care. I knew how to manage offices, evacuate patients, facilitate CPR classes, and deliver babies, but teaching middle school children was something I had never done before. The dynamics of running a classroom was not as it appeared on television. The theories and the practical applications were hardly what I imagined. While I struggled to grasp many of the concepts I was able to earn A's and B's in my courses and that really boosted my self-confidence!

It seemed that just like military jargon, there was a unique educational jargon. There was the DI, MI, IEP, PBL, CIA, and LRE to list just a few. We learned Bloom's Taxonomy and how to use it to get the most from students. We learned how differentiated instruction ensured that all students at every level were being challenged. While learning how to use an interest survey to identify learning styles I learned that I was a kinesthetic, analytical, and auditory learner. I used that knowledge subsequently to create assignments and projects that students would enjoy based on their own individual style of learning.

My professors were all passionate about the profession and about their students. They did not believe in shortcuts, and made sure that we knew the expectations of teacher preparation. We had a structured format which systematically taught us the keys to becoming a qualified and high-quality teacher. As students in a Christian university we had the added benefit of praying prior to the beginning of instruction and after class. These prayers were pivotal in my professional and spiritual life. After a few months I had found my rhythm. I was able to digest the concepts of teaching and apply them accordingly.

My first glimpse into a real live classroom was during a Level I practicum in Virginia Beach Public Schools, and Landstown Middle School was the perfect fit for me. My daughters were already attending Landstown Elementary School and the middle school provided me with a great opportunity. It was following this experience I knew for certain that I wanted to teach English at the middle school level. During my practicum, I had a bird's eye view of the most complex group of people in the world: pre-teenagers! I watched the teacher glide across the room as she solicited feedback from the eager learners. They had just finished reading Monsters on Maple Street and they really seemed to be enjoying it. The bell rang and in came another group of pre-teens. This time the students were far more vocal about their thoughts on the arrival of the Martians on Maple Street. Again, the teacher glided across the room in perpetual motion. She kept the students on task while maintaining an active learning environment. I sat there with a smile because I knew that one day soon I would be doing exactly the same sort of thing in my own classroom.

As the summer was quickly approaching, I prepared my resume in the hope of securing a teaching position for the upcoming school year. As I prepared to teach, I decided that I would relocate just about anywhere. I had begun to realize my purpose. As I continued my education I realized that God had a divine plan for my life and everything that I had gone through had led me to this place. And guess what - I was hired by Suffolk Public Schools as a 7th grade English and History teacher. It was a new position so I did not have to fill any shoes and to top it off I received a pay increase because of my military service. I was taken to what would be my new classroom. I was shown the library, the gym, and the teacher's workroom. I was on cloud nine, and I started my chosen career that fall.

There is an inescapable part of a new teacher's life that is called the unsolicited feedback. Some veteran teachers delight to give you feedback plus as much gossip as you would like to hear (in the teachers' lounge, of course). I was given quite a bit of advice on what to expect during my first year. "Your first year of teaching will be your worst year, statistics show if you can make it through the first three years, you will be more likely to continue in the profession", and my favorite, "you are going to have some big shoes to fill". I was the new teacher with the name nobody could pronounce! I remember my first open house. I wore a two-pieced blue and white seersucker dress and blazer set. The parents walked into my room to meet the new English teacher with the French name. In unspoken words, my presence was a relief for some parents and uncertainty for others. But after I had struggled through the evening I knew I had been sent to that school for a reason.

My first year was indeed my hardest of what is now almost ten years of teaching. It was a whirlwind, a distant memory, a blast, and a blessing all in one. I was assigned to a great mentor. She was on the 7th grade English team and she was my mentor for the whole of my first year. What I loved most about her was that she allowed me to be as creative as possible. If something did not work well, I discarded it and chalked it up to a learning experience. My mentor gave me an opportunity to learn for myself. She did not control my every move but allowed me the freedom to fail and in doing so, it was a valuable lesson. The seventh grade English Team was a tight knit group that was well structured and well organized. The team of women took me under their wings and with all of their years of expertise they led and guided me through the challenges that all new teachers face. They helped me lay a firm foundation for my future teaching.

The concepts that I had learned in the Career Switcher program unfolded once I was in the classroom. From the moment I stepped into my role as a teacher, I was able to take the curriculum and make it relevant for my students. I differentiated my instruction to meet the needs of all of my students. I discovered to my delight that I was gifted with classroom management skills and some veteran teachers would ask, "What school district were you in before coming to Suffolk"? "This is my first year teaching," I would reply. But I knew I was also extremely lucky: my school was well organized and we had a culture that was conducive for learning.

At any time of the day, administrators could walk into any classroom and find an active learning environment where students were actively engaged. In addition to my in-school mentor I was assigned a mentor by Regent University. She was a hugely experienced recently-retired veteran teacher who provided valuable feedback to help me improve my teaching. I had dynamic students who were eager to learn. As a first year teacher, I used formative and summative assessments, and project based learning to assess my students' level of understanding. I utilized cooperative learning and concept based teaching as a framework to develop critical thinking, and my mentor helped me to ensure that my instruction was rigorous and relevant. I developed lessons that were at the higher levels of Bloom's Taxonomy. I worked with many parents so that we operated as a team to meet the needs of the children. While I did experience a few disappointments and challenges in my first year, I was able to achieve passing scores for my students in English and in History standardized tests. My second year was even better; I was nominated for Suffolk's Wal-Mart Teacher of the Year. This accolade brought $1,000 to the school, a snap shot of yours truly in *The Virginian Pilot*, and a huge boost of self-confidence. At long last I had found my calling!

For the past nine and a half years, I have graded papers, written lesson plans, wiped tears, attended games, called parents, and mentored students. For every moment I was discouraged, overworked, and sometimes feeling unappreciated, there were many more moments of joy as I witnessed the 'Aha' look on the face of a child. I have the privilege of being a part of something so big I may never know the magnitude of it all, and as I look ahead I see myself as a player in the best free public education that a student can receive in a global society. I know this will require commitment, active engagement, determination, and continual improvement on my part. I relish the fact that

God saw fit to take someone like me and use me for His glory; I have the privilege of being a teacher whose mission is to see children succeed so that they have a smoother journey in the workplace than the one I experienced.

My grandmother inspired me. She was underprivileged and what some might call uneducated, but she could read, write, and had wisdom beyond measure. She helped me understand that the true value of an education would reach far beyond the years it would take to obtain one. A few weeks ago, a student said to me during the daily warm up "Ms. Bougouneau, you need to write a book about yourself". I might indeed do that one day, and perhaps some of what you have just read will form the first chapter

CHAPTER FOUR
My Eighth Life
by Dawn Florence

Ms. Florence entered the Career Switcher program in 2012 and she is currently teaching math at Norview Middle School in Norfolk.

IF SOMEONE HAD TOLD ME that one day I would be a middle school math teacher, I would have told them that they had lost their mind! Not only did I have no intentions of ever becoming a teacher, and why in the world would I ever want to spend seven hours a day trying to teach a bunch of adolescent preteens/teenagers anything?!? I hated my own middle school years, and the whole adolescent scenario of muddled hormones, years filled with uncertainty and insecurity, and way too much drama. I had no interest in reliving those transformational years in any form or fashion, let alone being on the frontline of trying to impart any type of learning upon these pubescent creatures! But guess what? At the age of 46 I am now in my third year of teaching 6th grade math, and I love it! How in the world did I get here?

What did I do before becoming a middle school teacher? The answer to that question is not a simple one. Yes, I am a career switcher, and a bit of a chronic one at that. You could call me a perpetual career switcher, and when people ask me what I do, I usually tell them that I am on my eighth life! My previous seven lives consisted of being a software engineer, college instructor, preschool computer teacher, stay-at-home mom/domestic engineer, substitute teacher, founder and president of a non-profit corporation, and office automation technician at an elementary school. Unlike many people, it took me over twenty years to finally figure out what I wanted to be when I finally grew up. What is truly amazing is that it was the journey through these many lives that prepared me to embrace this calling of teacher, and despite my resistance, it is now abundantly clear that I was destined to teach.

As the first born child of a retired elementary school teacher whose career spanned thirty seven years, and as the granddaughter of African-American sharecroppers whose education levels did not extend past the second grade, I grew up with the knowledge of the value of education in one's life. My love of learning and the gift of teaching run through my veins. The field of education has always been an integral part of my life as far back as I can remember. Surprisingly enough, however, teaching was never my first career choice as a child. The first recollection of my answer to the "What do you want to be when you grow up?" question was 'brain surgeon'. This response was when I was about five years old, and apparently I said that I wanted to be able to help people think better! As I reflect on the reasoning behind my early childhood ambition, it has become clear that even as a child I had an underlying desire to assist others in utilizing their minds to the best of their ability.

Despite my lackluster recollections about my own middle school years, I have always loved children. My first job at the age of ten was as a babysitter, and it continued to be my source of income throughout my teen years, but I did not discover my love of teaching until my early twenties. It was during a stint in the corporate world as a software engineer that I participated in a weekend program teaching high school students math and engineering. Though I made a hefty salary at my job, nothing in my position as a software engineer was as fulfilling as working with those young people and seeing the light bulbs of new knowledge illuminate in their eyes. I soon left the corporate sector and realized my passion for teaching as a community college instructor. Despite my salary being cut in half, the feeling of fostering student learning and providing guidance to young adults was exhilarating. I absolutely loved it!

Soon after I discovered my passion for teaching, I found an even greater passion as the mother of three young children. I poured my all into nurturing and teaching my family, and strived to instill in them the same desire for learning as my mother had instilled in me. As a military wife and mother, I chose to stay at home full-time with my children. I was still teaching, but now my children were my students and our home was their classroom. It was not until my youngest child went to school that I actually made my way back into a 'real' classroom as a substitute teacher, and I discovered what I thought was the best gig ever! As a substitute, I had the flexibility to choose if and when I wanted to work; I could still be available to my own children (I even saw them throughout the work day if I was subbing at their school!); and I got to do what I loved without all the responsibilities of being a full-time teacher. No lesson plans to create. No papers to grade. No parents to deal with. No administration looking over my shoulder. No need to return to the same class again if the students seemed horrible. And the true beauty of it all was that I could experience the joy of teaching and the thrill of being the 'fun substitute' that the children loved. It was perfect!! I would become a professional sub…or so I thought.

Around the time that my youngest child was in the 4th grade my husband, an officer in the US Navy, began talking about retirement. It was also the time that he began pressuring me about when I was going to get a 'real' job. My husband had long asserted that after working and supporting our family for many years, his plan after the Navy was to stay at home and take care of the children and play golf while I would go to work to provide financially for the family. Since I had been a software engineer in one of my previous lives, he was banking on the money-making potential that he had married. In the midst of my many lives, however, I had absolutely no idea what I would do next. Plus, after more than fifteen years of following my husband all over the world (Mobile, Alabama; Monterey, California; Norfolk, Virginia; San Diego, California; and Naples, Italy) to support his career, staying home with our children, and not working in the same job for more than a year or two, what credentials did I have? Who was going to hire me, and to do what? I had a Master's in Computer Science from the University of Pennsylvania, but it had been years since I even thought about doing anything in the subject which I had studied in college. What was I going to do? So began my search for what my eighth life would bring.

As a long term substitute teacher of 6th grade students I fell in love with the age group and I seemed to develop special connections with middle school students. My initial thought was towards becoming a guidance counselor, but as I researched various programs, I determined that it was going to be an arduous and expensive process for which I did not have the time or resources. I found that obtaining a provisional teaching certification would be a much more streamlined process and a much easier way to get my foot in the door. Plus, teachers are always in high demand with the turnover rate in the public school system. Furthermore, guidance counseling positions were few and far between whereas securing a teaching position appeared to be a more distinct, straightforward possibility and I could still have a positive impact on the youth of the community.

My journey to becoming a middle school teacher was a relatively smooth process. I researched Career Switcher programs and finally settled on a program that a dear friend of mine had successfully completed at Regent University. As I delved deeper into the program details, I learned that I could attain a provisional teaching license in as little as four months!! It was going to require going back to graduate school but I was not worried about that. I have been a chronic overachiever from as far back as I can remember, so being a student has always been my forte. My coursework began in January 2012 and by the June of that same year, I was hired!!

Life as a graduate student (this time as a wife and mother of three) was an intense time, but the instructors I had were phenomenal, and my fellow classmates were incredibly supportive. We worked together, striving for the common goal of getting that coveted teaching contract. There were two professors who had the most profound impact on me, and interestingly enough, they had quite different approaches to teaching. Additionally, their individual philosophies on how we should approach the profession as new teachers were in stark contrast. One professor, whom I will call 'Dr. Warm and Fuzzy' created a very personable and welcoming learning experience from day one of class. Dr. Warm and Fuzzy promoted a philosophy of meeting students where they are, ensuring that they are given the opportunity to express themselves and be responsible for their own learning. Dr. Warm and Fuzzy was a wealth of knowledge and created an environment that was compassionate, collaborative, and student-centered. The other professor, 'Dr. Strictly Business', did not crack a smile on the first night of class and established the boundaries of seasoned teacher/professor with us students from the first minute of class. Dr. Strictly Business was a firm believer in the 'don't smile until December' attitude when it came to interactions with students, and was a firm believer in setting clear guidelines for rules and procedures and consistently enforcing them. I gleaned a great deal from both professors, and was able to implement much of what I had learned when I started teaching in my own classroom.

In addition to coursework, the Career Switcher program required a practicum experience, during which I interacted with teachers working in the grade level and content areas that I hoped to teach. It was not quite student teaching, but more a golden opportunity to spend time in a real classroom situation, to shadow the cooperating teacher, to witness teaching in action, and to make observations about the various methods and strategies that were being implemented. My practicum experience was chock-full of examples of what worked and what did not work with regard to engaging students. One of the most important things that I learned during my practicum experience was that in order for students to learn, students must take ownership of their learning, and as a teacher it was my responsibility to encourage them. Many of the students that I encountered during my practicum did not have an intrinsic desire to learn and it knew it would be my job to not merely teach, but to motivate my future students so that they would want to learn. To provide extrinsic rewards and incentives for their initial successes would hopefully lead to them developing an intrinsic desire to succeed, even if they had never felt that way before.

To say that my first year of teaching was no picnic would be a gross understatement; it was actually a bit of a nightmare! Even though I had taught college students, preschoolers, and had been in several classrooms throughout my life, none of this had prepared me adequately for the eighty-some sixth grade middle school students who were placed in my charge on the first day of school in September, 2012. I don't know who was more nervous, me or the students. I had to keep reminding myself: I am the adult here, I really am the teacher. So I smiled and greeted my students at the door, I had a cute little 'getting to know one another' activity for them, and I had a cool PowerPoint presentation to share with them to introduce myself and welcome them all to our classroom. I wanted them to be excited about learning and to know that we were going to have fun learning in Mrs. Florence's 6th Grade Math Class. It was going to be a great school year…or so I hoped…

My first two classes on that first day went rather smoothly, but by the time the last class came, the students would not stop arriving in the room! For some reason I ended up with thirty-eight students on my roster, all of whom were trying to fit into a classroom with only thirty desks. I stood there in total unbelief and shock as I tried my best to get the students to settle down in order to get them to complete the initial activity I had prepared. There were students everywhere! They were all on top of each other, many with nowhere to sit, and I was expected to teach them something. I did not know what to do. I remember that for a moment I was just standing at the front of the classroom, spanning the room in a bit of a haze as the students all talked at the same time, and my attempts to quiet them down failed miserably. At that moment, despite all that I had learned, I felt that nothing during my teacher preparation coursework had equipped me for this scenario.

The next day I went to my principal to make him aware of the situation but he told me that schedules were being adjusted and until the changes were made that I would simply have to cope. This was not the response that I was expecting and it took me aback. I felt completely unsupported. The thought of not knowing how I was going to manage my last class of the day had me in tears. I recall returning to my classroom that afternoon, trying my best to provide direct math instruction to thirty-eight 6th graders who had just returned from a PE class. It was an absolute nightmare! Thank goodness for my Math Coach who learned of my distress and assisted me as best he could. If he had not, I fear I might have walked out that very day.

As the first week of school progressed, things did not get much better. As a matter of fact, they actually got worst. I was ready to quit by the end of that week. I was also struggling to find a semblance of balance as a working mom. I told myself that if I quit teaching I'd become a greeter at Walmart -- a simple job that did not require anywhere near the enormous demands required of a teacher. I was overwhelmed beyond belief with the paperwork, learning the curriculum, dealing with parents, managing student misbehavior, and the stress of knowing that an administrator could turn up in my classroom at any moment to observe and critique what I was doing. I had heard from many experienced teachers that what I was experiencing was normal and par for the course, but I felt like I was drowning and I could not envision it getting any better. Despite the advantage that I had of having spent three weeks as a long-term substitute at the school that hired me, my first week of being a full-time classroom teacher and responsible for my own classes was a truly daunting experience. How I wished that I just been a professional substitute teacher.

On top of the challenge of the demands of my new teaching job I found that I was in a bit of a culture-shock. I was teaching in a low-income, urban school district that was predominately African-American, but I had grown up in a middle class, predominantly white suburb. All my substitute teaching experiences had been in predominantly white, middle to upper class communities or in very diverse schools on a military base. So despite being an African-American woman teaching predominately African-American children, I was out of my element. The demographics of the students and their life experiences differed greatly from what I was familiar with. How was I going to reach these kids in order to teach them?

My students, especially a few of the African-American females, had very strong personalities and they constantly challenged my authority. Many of these young girls wanted to do what they wanted, and when they wanted to do it. They were barely teenagers, but it was clear that they thought we were all on the same level. It appeared that because I was a nice and friendly teacher, who smiled and encouraged them to express their opinions, they deemed that kindness for weakness. It was during my second week as a new teacher that one of these young ladies, with whom I had tried to enforce my expectations for classroom behavior, became angry, yelling and disrespectful. I reprimanded her and asked her to leave the classroom in an effort to maintain control and to ensure that the rest of the students knew who was in charge. In the midst of our back and forth, and to my utter shock and disbelief, this student physically pushed me. At this point I began to wonder seriously if teaching was really for me.

Shortly after this incident I broke down. I was barely surviving, and the stress was more than I thought I could bear. There was even one time, in the middle of the school day, that I packed up my things and told my principal that I did not think I could do it anymore. I felt like I was drowning and that it was in my best interest and the best interest of my students that I leave. I reached out to my Career Switcher administration and expressed that I did not think that I could continue with the program and that I wanted to find out how to withdraw. I felt defeated, and I did not believe that I was going to make it. I recall emailing the following to a fellow Career Switcher when asked if things were getting better:

> *No, not particularly...I've just been catatonic this last week, and trying to figure out if it can make it till June!! I'm drowning in paperwork; seems like half my kids are failing; and trying to teach when i spend half my time being a therapist, disciplinarian, surrogate parent, etc... on top of all the other gazillion things they want us teachers to do!!! It is just utterly exhausting....*

But I did make it to June and I completed my first year of teaching. Trust me, it was no easy task, and truly and uphill battle, but I had the support and guidance of some wonderful mentors from Regent's Career Switcher program. These veteran teachers came into my classroom and provided me with valuable advice and much needed encouragement They saw something in me and how I related with my students that I did not even see in myself. In addition to my university mentors, one of the members of my 6th grade math team was truly instrumental in helping me get through each day and constantly supported me in those moments when I thought I would fall. Additionally, my mother and father, who were my biggest cheerleaders, kept telling me that it would get better. With great wisdom, my mother reminded me to do what I could and to focus on reaching one student at a time.

As the school year progressed I began to see the impact I was making in the lives of my students. What I began to realize was that teaching was much more than delivering the subject matter and getting students to follow the classroom rules. Teaching was about building relationships and showing the students that I cared for them and valued who they were. Once I made this my focus it became clear that I was actually making a difference, albeit gradually. Many of the same girls who had given me such a challenging time at the beginning of the school year, even the student who pushed me (yes, she stayed in my class the entire school year), began to come by my classroom every morning to see me and to give me a hug. This let me know that I was finally reaching them; now I could not give up.

At the end of the school year when the results of our standardized test scores were released, it turned out that I had not done that bad of a job teaching. As the newest teacher on the 6th grade math team, I actually ended up having one of the highest pass rates. My students' assessments and benchmark exams had progressively improved from one quarter to the next, so clearly they were actually learning. The results of these standards of learning was the ultimate demonstration of the effectiveness of my teaching. But what was the most affirming to me was that on the last day of school, many of my students wrote "love notes" on the board saying 'We will miss you Mrs. Florence' and 'Mrs. Florence is the best teacher' and 'We love you Mrs. Florence.' I knew now that the students needed me; I had to return the next year.

I spent the majority of my first year of teaching either drowning or gasping for air so it was a relief it was to get to the last day of school in June. Despite how difficult my inaugural year of teaching had been, and how discouraging it was to tackle that 90 degree learning curve I had been faced with, something inside me said that I had to go back. I had finally caught my breath by the end of the school year and now I wanted to see if I could actually stay above water. Plus, I had learned so much that first year and had so many ideas of how I would do things differently the next time around, that the chronic overachiever in me took over. I was up to the challenge and I signed my contract for the next school year. I was going back for more!

What a difference a year makes. I had a great second year of teaching! I developed wonderful relationships with my students, I regularly experienced the lightbulbs of learning beaming throughout my daily lessons and I earned the respect and confidence of my colleagues and administrators. I took the potpourri of ideas I had gleaned, the advice I was given and the lessons learned from my many mistakes during my first year of teaching, and developed my very own classroom management system and style of teaching. I realized that I had to balance my loving, compassionate, and caring persona with a structured, respect-oriented, and high-expectations driven approach to create the best possible learning environment for all of my students. I had to meet each of my students where they were, treating each one as an individual person of value who was worthy of my respect.

In addition to having an entirely new outlook and a year of experience under my belt, my second year of teaching also brought along an entirely new administration. The new administrators were extremely supportive and truly wanted to make our jobs as teachers easier. There was a shift in the school's culture that truly put the needs of the students first by way of ensuring that the teachers had every resource available to create the best possible learning environment for students. The new administrators promoted teamwork and created an atmosphere of mutual respect and trust that made all the difference in the world for me. I no longer felt like I was drowning…I was actually treading water.

As my second year of teaching progressed, I can honestly say that I was truly getting the hang of teaching middle school math. Having become familiar with the curriculum in my first year, I was able to focus on creating interactive lessons to promote student engagement and to differentiate my instruction to ensure that all my students were learning. I had the opportunity to see the effectiveness of my teaching when one of my classes was swapped with another teacher's class. I was given an honors class whose assessment scores were not at the level expected, and because I had shown success with the honors class I was already teaching, I was charged with bringing this new class to a similar level. Within a matter of a few weeks, I was able to deliver instruction to my new students to achieve a 100% pass rate!! I then went on to finish the school year with 83% of my students passing their Standards of Learning exams! I was one proud teacher and thrilled that my students rose to the occasion; they had truly worked hard to achieve such a high pass rate.

In addition to my successes in the classroom, I also found the time and energy to bring my non-profit organization, Little Sistahs in the Know, Inc., to my school in the form of an after-school program. Very dear to my heart, Little Sistahs in the Know, is a program I had founded in a 'previous life' and which strives to build self-esteem and foster a positive self-image in African-American girls through literature, culture, history, and community service. My experiences during my first year of teaching with my African-American female students made it clear to me that there was a need for this type of programming at my school. I saw this as an opportunity to further impact the lives of my students, above and beyond everyday classroom experiences. The support and encouragement that I received from my administration and fellow colleagues in the implementation of this program was tremendous. All in all, my second year as a middle school teacher was an awesome! I was a finally swimming.

The old adage, 'the third time's a charm' could not be any more true than when it comes to my third year of teaching. My first week of school in year three was truly a stark contrast to the harrowing first week during my first year of teaching. I entered my third year with a level of self-assuredness that I could have never imagined during those challenging early days. I was implementing a classroom management system that I knew worked, I had a relatively solid grasp of the curriculum, and I had developed instructional strategies that were proven to be effective. Furthermore I had earned the confidence of my principal who continued to be a strong supporter of my non-profit organization's after school program and who had now selected me to be the leader of the 6th grade math team. For someone who never had any plans of becoming a teacher, let alone a middle school teacher, things were going pretty well.

As I progress through my third year of teaching, I continue to enjoy the thrill of the 'Aha!' moments of my students when they finally understand a concept. I welcome the morning hugs from those students who just the day before had misbehaved or were disrespectful. I cherish the joy of knowing that I am truly making a difference in the lives of young people. As I reflect on my adventurous journey to become a middle school teacher, I know that although it is an exhausting, demanding, and highly underpaid profession, the impact that I am making on today's youth makes it all worth it. You could say that I have settled nicely into this, my eighth life! I do not know how long I will be here but in the meantime I plan to keep swimming along strongly as a middle school teacher in these ever changing, often unpredictable, and sometimes tumultuous seas.

CHAPTER FIVE
Marching to a Different Drumbeat
by Teresa Habib

Ms. Habib entered the Career Switcher program in 2012 and she is currently teaching music and chorus at Glenwood Elementary School in Virginia Beach.

HAVE YOU EVER TAKEN one of those personal traits inventories? You know the ones, you are invited to rate yourself in the various different categories and see where the majority of your traits end up. I must have taken at least five of these, and after the first two I even thought of altering my responses because I thought it would be fun and interesting to get a different result about myself! But alas, I always landed smack dab in the middle of the servant-style leadership category. Perhaps there is a reason for this and I just did not want to see it at the time.

At the time of writing this chapter I have been teaching elementary music in a public school for two years. I work at a very large school with approximately 950 students in grades K-5, and I personally teach 750 of them….each week. No, I have not yet memorized all their names but I am honest-to-goodness still trying!! The Career Switcher program was a major factor in my surviving that first year of teaching, and the most valuable tools that kept me going were the resources and the people. Resources included the bible which offered invaluable help for every single day, the Wong and Wong textbook that offered invaluable help for the first days of school, and the graduate level classes that prepared me. The people I met through Regent gave me a renewed faith in kindness and honest to goodness…well, goodness. My professors were true educators. My assigned Regent mentor during the whole of that first year was a ray of sunshine and support. Her vast experience in the field of education is extraordinary, and combined with a southern sense of humor she gave me reassurances and validation that the experiences in my previous life really did give me the skills to survive, and to thrive, in this new adventure.

Although I am now in the second year of my second career I have to remind myself daily that my responsibility is not only to introduce music into the lives of my students, but to educate the children and to assess their learning. During the first year I was really focused on the curriculum and its objectives. Yes, even music has those requirements and they are very stringent but I am now confident that the children I am responsible for learn that music makes them smarter, they learn that I really do care about them, and they learn that they are expected to do their best at all times. In my classes they learn that music has a very long history and they are part of tomorrow's history; they learn how to dance and sing; they learn to share and to care about one another in my classroom. How do I know this? I know this because they tell me and because they show me.

As a music teacher I have the ability to measure learning in a very subjective manner. For example, can my five-year olds keep a steady beat? Since keeping a steady beat is a curriculum objective in kindergarten, I can assess their learning by watching them march around the room to a fun song. Or for differentiation I can have them play on a maraca or a pair of claves. The sky is the limit and I am fortunate that I can watch and assess without any paper and pencil. However, the older the student, the less subjective I can be. For example; my fourth and fifth graders must actually create music, and that requires tangible evidence. I can see if they are learning by what they write or draw, and I base my feedback on that data.

There are other ways for me to identify if learning is or is not taking place -- I allow my students to become a teacher. If they can explain and demonstrate a new skill to me or to another student, then I can attest to the learning. The obvious methods include pencil to paper, as well as having exit tickets or using available technology in the classroom to check learning. Role-playing, when possible, is one of my favorite ways to see if they truly understand a concept. We role-play for actual skill activities, and we role-play for personal conflicts. To me, teaching is not all about the objectives in the book, but rather the objectives in life. Life experience is what makes Career Switcher teachers so special.

When it comes to assessing for specific skills, I am still deciphering the best way to set up my learning plan in order to gradually increase students' confidence and relevance to the testing material. I do not know how the general education teachers do it, and I am not yet sure I am doing it correctly. Not every class gets a good grade on the big quarterly assessments, and I am constantly going back to the drawing board to fix my approach. If they didn't learn, it is my fault. That was something I learned in the Career Switcher courses and I really believe it!

The first year of school is difficult for all new teachers, and Career Switchers are no exception. Mine felt like I had been dropped into a giant sea full of young students with a deflated lifesaver, and my Regent mentor was holding that rope that kept me from drowning completely. As a music specialist I had no other person in my building to guide me. I was the one and only! I was asking questions all over the place at the risk of damaging my ego. For example: how in the world do you work this copier and what is a pass code and do I have one? The questions were endless, and the ones I did not ask were the ones that seemed to matter the most. The lessons I learned quickly included being unafraid to ask all the questions, no matter how trivial they may have seemed.

I learned to request a school-building mentor, an experienced person to walk around the building with me during the first few days to show me the layout, instruct me what to during a fire drill, and to inform about other necessities such as where to eat lunch or to get a cup of coffee. I also learned quickly to make maximum use of the mentor assigned by the university. We are all professionals in our own way and the mentor who is a retired teacher has a wealth of background experience and the flexibility of time in order to share experience with a novice teacher.

So how did I become that novice teacher? Preparing to be a teacher through Regent University was an enjoyable experience. The yearlong academic focus was just challenging enough to keep me totally interested, yet not so overwhelming that I felt like giving up because of the demands of a busy life. The 'gearing up for the classroom' courses have proven to be the most useful and I am still using the textbooks and remembering the hints and advice given by the professors. I refer to Wong and Wong on a regular basis, and their textbook is sitting right beside my miniature bible verses that help me get through some special days. I was warned there would be challenging days and I haven't been disappointed, but I feel well equipped to handle whatever comes my way.

The Praxis II exams were no joke. I passed the music exam the first time and that was a relief. The second assessment I attempted, English for middle and high school grades, took a couple of tries but it was well worth the effort. With two Praxis II subjects under my belt I became more marketable while looking for jobs because I could apply for both English and music positions. I figured if I was going to be a teacher, I should stick to what I am passionate about. That way I enjoy going to the school building each day and it doesn't have to feel like work.

Bur how did I get excited about becoming a teacher in the first place? Well, I should have seen it coming! At 17 I joined the Marine Corps to become a professional musician. During my high school years I was often tasked with teaching the younger students in music, and throughout my military career I was assigned to teach at all levels and locations. For example, I was assigned two tours at the tri-service school of music as an instructor, and in each of my units for 21 years I was one of the educators in all aspects of training. I delivered courses to large numbers of marines, and I was trained to the highest level of musical leadership and was given teaching roles in every unit to which I was assigned. This was not the normal route for young enlisted members, but apparently I gave the impression early on that I could teach and wasn't afraid to do it. I never even considered that the experience of these years would turn out to be a portent of things to come.

Fast-forward 21 years. I was now retired and going to school fulltime. For the first time in my adult life I was under no contract, no commitment, and I could live anywhere in the world and do anything I wanted. Wow, what a feeling! I worked diligently towards finishing my undergraduate degree that I had started ten years previously, and I also became a substitute teacher. The situation was working out just fine, but I still tell people that God must have a sense of humor. Sometimes we can control our destiny and make decisions, but sometimes not. My plans changed drastically when my retirement present arrived about 9 months after I began my new life and career path – a new son arrived in the world!

My undergraduate degree was a focus on psychology and counseling. My plan was to become a licensed counselor or school counselor and I had just entered the graduate counseling program at a local university. Once my little joy arrived, I realized I could no longer sacrifice time with my son for the insane amount of unpaid internship hours required to become a licensed counselor. To clarify, I did not want nor desire to gain a degree in music education or performance. It was redundant for me at this point. My life and job experiences far outweighed anything I would learn or experience in a college setting. I had traveled the world playing music and was a top-rated performer with recording credits already to my name and so a music degree from a college held no interest for me. I wanted something different. I will always have music in my soul but I wanted some way to reinvent myself. I was no longer challenged, and when a military member transfers to civilian life, the stakes have changed. I had to do something new to validate my existence, and that something for me became teaching.

I had sworn to myself previously that I would never teach professionally (I also swore I would never own a minivan, but that's beside the point!). I heard too many times the cliché, "those who can, do, and those who can't, teach." I had already proven myself as a professional musician and post-secondary educator of sorts, and maybe the competitive side of me wanted another challenge. Teaching had been my life, in a very unorthodox capacity, for over 20 years. I thought I had taught enough.

Enter children, stage left; they are the real reason I teach. They are the light of my daily life and the reason I get up every morning. They are also the reason I drink more coffee than ever before. They are the reason I keep my textbooks close by and my bible closer. Teaching is not something I want to do, it has become something I now have to do. I tried to leave. I tried to break away in order to try something different. I tried to change my servant-style leadership traits. Yet here I am, fully credible in the civilian world as a real educator. I am a servant to the education of kids. I stand in as a surrogate parent to them, a counselor, an ear, a hug, a smile and the boundary maker. At different times of the day I am all these things packed into one. My military time holds no candle to the work of teachers. Deployments and combat are tough, but the sad, destitute lives of some innocent children are far worse. They come to school for their own reasons. Not always to learn, but sometimes to have something to eat, sometimes to find a responsible adult to tell them no, or to accept them in all their crazy ways. Teachers, good teachers, will see past the curriculum and testing to the child underneath the dirty clothes, empty stomachs, sassy attitudes and trouble-making spirits.

Good teachers will get children to learn while giving them the strict boundaries they need and the encouragement they might lack. Education is not in a book- it is in the heart. What an amazing and humble place to be. I will continue on this journey as God sees fit, and as for long as I am able to be a positive role model and influence on these little lives that are our future.

CHAPTER SIX

Always Listen to Your Nearest and Dearest
by Kevin Houck

*Mr. Houck entered the Career Switcher program in 2010 and he is currently
teaching math at Lake Taylor High School in Norfolk*

I HAVE TO DEDICATE THIS CHAPTER to my wife, Rachel,
without whom I would never have had the wherewithal to become a
Career Switcher. I had graduated from Old Dominion with a degree in
Business in the fall of 1995. I had been working at a quick-print shop and
had worked my way up to become the Store Manager right before I graduated.
The owner of the business was located in Raleigh, North Carolina and had a
string of these shops near Duke, the University of North Carolina and North
Carolina State. My shop was located across from Old Dominion University.
Right after I graduated the owner decided he wanted to divest himself of the
ODU store and offered to sell it to me. I was both thrilled and scared at the
opportunity! I had worked at the shop for nine years and knew exactly how
it was run. I had worked my way up the ladder starting as a Key Operator
which was a glorified term for customer representative, to Night Manager, to
Assistant Manager, and then to Store Manager. I knew the business but now
the pressure of bottom line sales and profits would be on me. My wife and I
talked it over and we were able to work out the financial deals to enable me
to take over as the owner.

In the summer of 1993 my oldest son, Aaron, was born. In the fall of 1998
we registered our son at St. Gregory the Great Catholic School in Virginia

Beach. My wife had gone to the school to finish up the paper work and when she got home she told me that Aaron was registered and that, by the way, she had registered me to be the coach of a soccer team at St. Gregory's. I remember wondering if she was somewhat crazy! I had never coached soccer, I knew little about the rules of the game, and my playing experience consisted of kicking the ball around a few times in grade school back in the 60's. Long story short, I was able to attend some licensing courses and obtain a "D" license in coaching and learned the nuances of a game that has now become my favorite sport. I was privileged to coach my son Aaron's team from recreation level to advanced level to travel level as he progressed through his high school education. My younger son, Nathan, four years younger than Aaron followed in his footsteps and I was able to coach him in soccer the same way as he progressed through high school. Unbeknownst to me, I was developing the ability to coach kids of all skill levels with the aim of moving to the highest levels of the game. I was dealing with parental issues and concerns and coaching very competitive and successful teams. My wife began to say to me that she thought I should go into teaching because I had a gift with the children and their parents. I wondered once more if she was crazy. Me, a teacher? I had never entertained the thought for one day as I grew up and eventually graduated from college. Besides, I owned my own business and transitioning to a new career would be too difficult.

Well, the first seven years of owning my own business went quite well. I increased sales and profits each year and grew the business to the point of having a printing press with an employee press operator. He was actually the parent of one of the boys I had coached for years so it seemed like it was meant to be. However, as the economy began its downturn in the early to mid-2000s my business began to decline. I had a good relationship with Old Dominion University and knew many of the department heads and professors who brought me much business. However, the university decided to open its own print shop and began to mandate that all department's keep their work in-house. This was really the beginning of the end for me as about

75% of my business was university related. I began to realize that I was going to have to close my business. I was so scared. What was I going to do? I had invested so much time and money and did not even know the process to close a business. Fortunately, I had been advised at the beginning of my business venture to obtain a good lawyer and a good accountant. Thank God I heeded that advice. I needed both these professionals and they helped me close the business as painlessly as possible in the summer of 2008. I began to think that maybe my wife wasn't so crazy after all and maybe I should go into teaching. As my business was closing I had spoken to the Career Switcher and Troops to Teacher departments at Old Dominion University. I had been doing a lot of printing for them so I was familiar with the process of transitioning to teaching.

However, I still did not think I would make a great teacher and decide to go to work in a management capacity for another print shop. In my heart, I knew it was not the job I wanted but I was too scared to try to change careers. As the following year progressed, I began working 50-70 hour weeks for this successful print shop but I was making less than half the money I had earned as the owner of my own shop. The hours and demands began to put a lot of stress on both of us and I began to cut back on coaching soccer. I was not happy in my job which was affecting my personal life; I had to make a drastic change. I needed to get as far away from the printing business as possible. When you own your own business you are driven by bottom line results. Are you making a profit or not? It is as simple as that. During the first seven years that I owned the business it was profitable. As such, I was able to grow the business and increasingly offer my employees regular raises, health insurance and a small retirement plan -- benefits that are really hard to offer for small businesses, and I took great satisfaction in being able to offer them to my employees. Unfortunately, when my business began to decrease I had to take away these expensive outlays. As my business began to decrease even further I was just trying to make payroll every two weeks while also trying to find rent and lease payments on my equipment. It became overwhelming and exhausting. My escape was coaching my soccer teams. I really enjoyed the teaching of the tactical and technical skills to the boys and seeing them use those skills and become successful on the field. I did not realize it at the time but teaching seemed to be in my blood.

So you now probably understand that wife was the sane person in our marriage and it was me who the crazy one. I had been working with kids of all ages for years while coaching and had been successful at it and, most importantly, I loved doing it. I decided right then and there that I was going to become a math teacher. I went to an open house at Regent University. I knew what Old Dominion University's Career Switcher program was all about and wanted to compare the two. Regent's information evening blew me away and when I went and chatted with the program chair I knew that Regent was for me. I registered for the summer 2010 Career Switcher course, and began my exciting journey into teaching.

Taking the Career Switcher program over the summer semester is a whirlwind of activity because so much is done in a relatively short amount of time. We overlapped a little bit with some of the Career Switchers who had joined the previous spring and it was nice to listen to their experiences and recommendations on how to handle certain classes, classroom management etc. The courses were extremely informative and exciting and the teachers at Regent were knowledgeable and genuinely excited to meet and teach us. Because it was a small group we really had time to get to know our professors which is so important. Meeting fellow Career Switchers and hearing their reasons for switching fields was equally fascinating. Our group members were all experiencing the same change in our lives so it really brought us close together. In addition, much of the work assigned to us involved small group projects so we spent time together collaborating which was so valuable. It allowed everyone to share their concerns and feelings as traveled together on our journey. We could support, commiserate, or just listen to one another. It was the summer of 2010 and the World Cup soccer tournament was underway. A couple of my fellow classmates were also avid soccer fans, so we really bonded!

The one thing I would have welcomed was more opportunity to practice teaching before getting hired teaching. I did do part of a week during my practicum but since it was in June the SOLs had been taken and the school's classes were really winding down. The classroom teacher allowed me to sit in and even teach a lesson but the children's sense of urgency was not there – they were thinking about vacation time! That is my only regret about taking the class in the summer semester as taking it in fall or spring allows more opportunity for teaching experience. As we wound down our Career Switcher Level One training the excitement of trying to get our first job heightened. It was wonderful to share in the happiness our classmates felt when they accepted their first teaching job. It was frustrating for those of us (and I was one of them) who did not get hired before 2010-2011 school year began. Eventually I did secure that coveted first teaching job, but it was neither where I envisioned it would be nor when I envisioned I would be starting.

You see I had it all planned out. I would graduate in August with my Career Switcher license and I would have a job teaching by the beginning of September. However, plans do not always work out the way they are designed! I did graduate with my Career Switcher license in August but I did not have a job teaching at the beginning of September. I began to get a bit frantic and expanded my job search beyond the Norfolk/Virginia Beach/ Chesapeake/Suffolk area. I included Hampton/Newport News/ Williamsburg/New Kent County and Northampton County on the Eastern Shore. I figured that I needed that first job, that first opportunity, and I would be willing to drive to get it. Since I did not have a job my wife suggested that I pursue my Master's in Education at Regent University, so I registered for two online courses. Word to the wise…marry a woman who is as smart as my wife…. it makes life so much more simple! I probably would have just sat there and stewed over the fact that I did not have a job. Instead, I kept my mind occupied with my coursework while still searching for a job. September came and went. No job offers arrived, although I did interview for a middle school math position in Williamsburg. October crept by...still nothing. My online courses were the only thing keeping me sane. I had to focus on them and not the fact that I was unemployed. Finally, at the beginning of November I received a call from Northampton County on the Eastern Shore of Virginia. They were in need of a 7th grade math teacher. I drove over for the interview and I was quite nervous. The interview went well, I thought. They threw a curve ball at me, though...they gave me a scenario and told me to teach them a math lesson on properties. So I got up and did so. I was so nervous I remember that I mixed up the associative and commutative properties. So, there I was thinking that the other part of the interview went well but I blew the impromptu lesson on properties. I thought there was no way they would hire a teacher for 7th grade math who does not know properties. I was crestfallen. The interview concluded and they told me they had more interviews more to conduct and would then make a decision. As I was leaving the office, however, the school principal who had sat in on the interview told me she really enjoyed my lesson! It had been so long since she had learned properties that she wouldn't have known if I had mixed the properties up one way or the other! Three days later I received a call from Northampton County and they offered me the job and wanted me to start the following Monday.

I was told that the teacher I was replacing would be in my class for the first two weeks to help ease me into the class and he would provide the first few lesson plans. So I showed up to work on the following Monday, November 11th 2010...my official first day of teaching. The outgoing teacher introduced me to the class and immediately turned the class over to me!! He had no lesson plans and nothing prepared; apparently he was under the assumption that had done the preparation. So I asked him what unit they were on, rolled up my sleeves, and began teaching with the textbook. It turned out that the teacher I was replacing was not currently endorsed in any discipline and he was trying to earn his endorsement in English. He had taught the class for three weeks while the division was searching for a qualified replacement. He in turn had replaced a previous teacher -- he had been moved to a position within the local high school. So I became the third teacher these students had in three months.

Needless to say, I had some behavioral issues. The students must have figured that I would not stick around any longer than my predecessors so a number of them decided to test me. I turned to my classroom discipline handbook and began trying to implement various strategies together with their consequences. I learned quickly that I had to choose ones that worked with my particular temperament rather than just pick haphazardly. I had one particular student who really tested the boundaries. I tried many different ways to deal with his behavior, including talking to his parents; nothing seemed to work. To this day I don't know what it was but when he realized that I was going to be there for the long haul and that I was not going to let his behavior go unchecked he began to work and his grades improved. He ended up transferring to another school two months after I began teaching his class and his parting words to me I will always remember were: "You know, Mr. Houck....you're alright. I'm going to miss your class!" He had been my first major challenge, I had overcome the problem, and I will never forget him and what he said.

Fortunately, Northampton County placed me with the math specialist for the district and she really assisted me with formatting lesson plans. In addition, I was mentored by a veteran 6th grade math teacher who dispensed invaluable assistance. I knew my students were doing well based upon questions they asked me during direct instruction. In general, they asked thought-provoking questions that indicated a basic level of understanding of the concepts. I used math warm ups to gauge previously taught material. Guided practice and independent practice were tools I used to help identify strengths and weaknesses that students demonstrated on a daily basis. These were generally informal assessments, and exit tickets were used to provide a quick check on student comprehension. These exit tickets were sometimes used as quiz grades, but the students knew when the exit ticket was a quiz because I would inform them. Finally, I used test scores to measure student progress. Quizzes and tests were the formal assessments I gave after monitoring all the informal assessments on a daily and weekly basis.

I had 57 students my first year of teaching and 52 of them passed the SOLs with four earning perfect scores and 12 having advanced scores. That worked out to be a 91% pass rate. Not bad for a first year teacher who happened to be the third math teacher these students had that year. I credit my success with the children having a strong sixth grade math teacher the previous year, the help from my mentor, excellent support from Northampton County Public Schools, and a lot of moral support from my wife. I began to realize that teaching was what I wanted to do for the rest of my working life and I was cautiously optimistic that I just might be good at it!

Looking ahead requires one to also look behind. It is hard to believe but I am currently in my fifth year of teaching. When I began as a Career Switcher I wanted to do middle school math and that is what I was initially endorsed in. I was wisely advised that if I wanted to stay a qualified middle school math instructor that I had better get my high school math endorsement as more and more middle schools are offering Algebra and Geometry in middle school. It took me a couple of tries but I finally earned my high school math endorsement. My goal, however, was to remain in a middle school and teach Algebra which is my favorite math course.

I moved from Northampton County Public Schools for logistical reasons at the end of my first year. I had about a 70 minute commute each way to the Eastern Shore and I was spending a lot of money on gasoline. In addition, a round trip through the Chesapeake Bay Bridge-Tunnel was $17 each day for tolls and I could not justify staying. I loved the math team and my administration so it was bittersweet when I had to leave but they all understood. I was then hired by an independent school which allowed me to teach closer to home. No big expenses, but also no benefit package! So after a year there I moved back to a public school position in Virginia Beach but unfortunately it was only a one year commitment. Tired of looking for a new job every summer I moved next to a high school position teaching Algebra in Norfolk (I decided high school would be fine after teaching high school geometry during summer school), and that is where I currently teach.

Each of my previous teaching jobs has provided me invaluable experience. They have shaped me and helped me to decide what I want to teach and where I want to teach it. I enjoy teaching Algebra - it is the foundation for high school math and higher mathematics. I see so many students struggling because they have not been given enough math in middle school and are ill-prepared for the challenges of Algebra. One day my journey may take me back to middle school to try and close some of those gaps. It may take me to the position as a math specialist to assist others and identify new ways to teach the subject. However, I know that whatever road it is it will be the right road for me because it involves teaching and teaching math – my wife had been correct! The feeling of making a difference in children's lives on a daily basis is why I went into teaching and that's why I intend to remain there.

CHAPTER SEVEN
The Making of an Educator

&

Tips for Educators in the Making

by Matthew Koeppen

Mr. Koeppen entered the Career Switcher program in 2009 and currently teaches science at Northside Middle School in Norfolk

TEACHING IS A CAREER often undervalued by American society, yet time spent as a student has a profound and undeniably life-long effect on every single person. In my journey to become a Career Switcher, I have traveled a rocky road of achievements, failures, joys, and false promises. Each of these factors has affected my teaching career in some manner, but throughout it all, the needs of the learners have always come first. The children we teach are the ultimate stakeholders, and everything else in teaching is of secondary importance. The guiding question for any educator, new or seasoned, is rather simple: 'how does (insert your topic here) benefit the children?' If that question cannot be answered easily, then why is this activity occurring? As you read this chapter you will discover how important it is for a teacher to try to be in the shoes of the students being taught, but first let me share a bit of my pre-career switcher life.

I was raised in a one bedroom apartment on Long Island by a single parent in a blue collar town that was way past its heyday. School was a bore for me, and I despised having to attend - what an irony considering my current career! Summers spent on the beaches of Fire Island were my refuge, only then I was free. Time spent in school eventually became prison-like even though I was a gifted at-risk middle school student without major disciplinary problems. The school system simply watched me stumble and fall from being a top performer into a downward spiral of cutting classes and ultimately a conversation with an assistant principal. He gave this 16-year-old two choices: quit or get kicked out. What a fool I was for allowing that administrator to convince me to quit! No intervention was ever provided. I do not share this out of resentment, but this experience allows me to see the warning signs among my students and to be the mentor to them that I never had.

About a year and a half later, I entered a multi-district night school pilot program designed as a 'catch all' for ex-students like myself, as well as for pregnant teens, drug offenders, and anyone else who was unable or unwilling to attend day school. We were a tight ragtag group, rebellious in our own ways, and for the first time I encountered a teaching staff dedicated to treating us with respect. Those teachers truly cared, they inspired us all to be successful, and I was graduated from high school a year later. Today I use that same model of caring and respect to educate the children in my own classroom.

By the time I was the legal age to work, I had already been mowing lawns and doing other odd jobs. My first long-term career began as a dishwasher in a local restaurant. The food service industry was always like an old friend to me and no matter what I did professionally, I always remained with it and earned extra money as long as I worked hard. After high school, the time had arrived for me to finally venture out on my own as a young adult. I escaped to 'The Hamptons' and was involved in the horticulture field in addition to food service. That lasted several years from my time as a delivery driver in one company to becoming the lead foreman in landscape construction at another. Oh, the people I have met and the vast estates I have seen! Those experiences taught me that no matter who someone is, or what level of society they associate with, people are people and they are either nice or they are not. They also taught me the subtleties of dealing with people at any level, an important skill that serves me well as an educator. A severe injury eventually forced me to make yet another change, and I enrolled in a community college without any clear direction other than an initial interest in business.

During my career, yes career, as a college student, immersion was my mantra and I embraced every experience I could through various organizations and societies. The ultimate accolade was serving as the New York region's president of the Phi Theta Kappa International Honor Society, and to this day I am still actively involved with the alumni association. Eventually my experiences in community college led me to seek a B.B.A. in Marketing from The College of William and Mary, and I then entered the white collar world of marketing, advertising, and sales.

My successes in the business world still left a gap in my life, and the reason I became a Career Switcher only became clear after further medical complications, relocating to another state, and taking the time during remission to reflect on who I was and what road I should travel. Hindsight provided me the realization that almost everything I had accomplished professionally and personally blazed the trail to become an educator. My beacon had been lit decades ago but it took me over twenty years to finally see it. The obvious choice based on my previous experience was to become an entrant into the world of education as a business education instructor; I wanted to enter a career and life of service. However, there were still numerous reservations about changing careers yet again. Reflecting on twenty years of food service, several of horticulture, and several more in the white collar world was a great run, but I did not want to fail while attempting something new.

So what better way to see if you like something than to 'try it before you buy it'! Although it took several months to secure a position as a substitute teacher with the local school district, it afforded me the best method of testing the waters. Being a daily substitute was interesting to say the least. Most school children are use to a substitute coming in and doing little or nothing. I was not that substitute, and I expected the learners to complete their assignments. Having a strong work ethic was necessary for them to emulate. The experience was rewarding, but extremely exhausting and late afternoon naps when returning home became the norm.

As a daily substitute you flip-flop between multiple schools and there is little time for relationship building, so it was important for me to draw on my sales experience by networking with office staff in order to be invited back. You carve out your reputation on a school-by-school basis. My reputation was that of a great performer. Eventually I was requested to start showing up automatically at one of the high schools each day, and a short while later I was offered a long-term substitute position which I gladly accepted. It was just the break I needed to try out being an educator.

Time spent as a long-term substitute allowed me to engage students on a daily basis and to develop relationships in a deeper and richer capacity. It was no longer like the first day of school every time I entered the classroom, and I was able to truly educate. Students respected me, my classroom procedures, and the expectations I had for them. Student work was submitted and graded, the grades were entered, and after school tutoring occurred. I helped students to turn their weaknesses into successes and everything seemed to click professionally. My 'ah ha' moment had finally occurred! I thought to myself how enjoyable and rewarding the experience was – I had finally found a career worth pursuing, and I needed to become qualified.

Preparing to become an educator was initially fast and furious. I was referred by a local school district to a Career Switcher program which was being offered at a few area colleges. The program was well suited for someone like myself who had professional experience in the working world, but who did not have the time to take on an additional four-year degree to become a teacher. Quite frankly, a four-year wait would have ended my exploration into education then and there. The good news was that program was close to home, it was at the graduate level, and it offered me an opportunity to complete half the credit hour requirements for a M.Ed. within four months. Luckily for me some courses were even offered online or in a hybrid format with on-campus and online meetings. To sweeten the deal, the state provided a grant to subsidize the program's tuition, and further financial incentive was offered by the local school district. I was ready!

Transitioning into the world of education would not have been feasible without the Career Switcher program. During my time in the private sector I had hired, trained, retained, and fired numerous employees. None of that mattered because those employees were adults who were expected to perform their assigned duties or become unemployed - training was expected to be completed. Those same expectations are present in education but the big difference is that children require motivation. The program taught me how to teach children through targeted goals based on state-mandated curriculum, how to assess informally and formally, how to create meaningful lesson plans, and most importantly, to appreciate how children think, act, and feel. Child and Adolescent Growth and Development was one of the most important courses I completed, as it rounded out the applied psychology courses taught during my business education. I discovered that turning a student's extrinsic motivation into intrinsic motivation is an important key to academic successes.

After completing phase one of the Career Switcher program successfully, I luckily landed a position as business education instructor at a middle school. That first year went by at lightning speed, and at times it seemed overwhelming. In order to manage, I drew on my previous experiences in time management, relationship management, customer service, networking, training, relevant personal stories, and numerous other knowledge, skills, and abilities from the private sector. I also valued the support of my mentor and the assistance and advice of other teachers. In addition to being in charge of a classroom, there was still district-level training and the Career Switcher phase two seminars on my plate. It was an extremely busy year, but at the end of it I was awarded my full five-year renewable license – it had all been worthwhile! That first year of teaching is probably the most difficult for all new teachers, so for those reading this chapter who might be considering a transition into teaching, I have a few nuggets to share with you that I hope might prove helpful.

Teaching is time well spent, but spend your time wisely. Time management is the key to any fruitful career, and one I have battled with for several years. During my time in the private sector the day ended when I left work and any unfinished tasks were simply rolled over with the exception of special projects or hard deadlines. I felt artful in completing multiple tasks and exceeding expectations set by myself or management; my day ended with a sense of satisfaction and I went home. As an educator your time is precious and it can easily consume your private life if you are not careful. Set a schedule and stick to it. Grading, lesson planning, creating ancillary lesson materials, and numerous other tasks are all time consuming. Your success as an educator equates to the quality of time you invest, not the quantity.

Respect all in the school building from the students to your peers. Students who feel respected will work for you and will embrace the lessons you present. Colleagues who are respected will share materials and advocate for your success behind the scenes. Failure to give respect may cause numerous hardships and suffocate the teaching and learning process.

Working as a member of a team of teachers may depend on the size of the school; if there a large number of staff teamwork may be the norm. My experience has led me to be a team of just one person for multiple subject preparations. If you are lucky enough to be placed on a collaborative team covering the same subject, then the workload is much easier to manage. I have seen great teams, but I have also experienced dysfunctional teams. My advice is to try to work with colleagues that you know will try to support you just as fully as you support them.

Data analysis is a driving force behind ensuring each student has a deep and rich understanding of the state standards, and it is a primary method to determine student success. Being data rich and information poor is a problem faced in all industries, and education is no different. Merely teaching course materials is much different than ensuring mastery of learning; transforming data into a usable format is as simple or complicated as a district makes it. I have not spoken with a single educator from any district who uses a program which paginates student grades, tests, and other data to a usable format, rather data are spread out among various programs. It is the teacher's task to create the filter that can provide the appropriate depth and breadth to provide timely and relevant data. I have experienced several trends in data extrapolation and analysis thus far. I adhere to mandates, of course, but what works best for me is to segment students into red, yellow, and green categories for each topic based on their test performance. Use a scoring range to define each category and it will help you to target individual students and small groups who need remediation. An area or areas in which all or most students are deemed red clearly requires an adjustment to your methodologies and approach.

Staying current in your teaching discipline is so very important. When I heard the story about the educator who let his transparencies 'turn yellow', it became clear that complacency is a risk. Although the story had referenced a technologically dated platform, it provided me with a cautionary tale to always remain current in my field. That logic applies to anyone in any field who wishes to be successful. However, there is a stark contrast between staying current and starting from scratch each year. Over time there are certain activities or approaches to the teaching and learning process which should not be changed because they succeed, but the best educators still seek to fine tune and hone their lessons no matter how effective they are.

Review, review, and then review some more. Exposure to anything multiple times activates and grows dendrites in the brain, an approach that has proven especially effective in the world of advertising. Cutting through the constant bombardment of products and services is a tough proposition and the science behind applied psychology is sound. Similarly, students need to review frequently. A constructivist scaffold of learning that includes an initial introduction, a review, then more familiarity, followed by greater insight and more reviews, will lead to ultimate mastery of the topic. Connecting the dots from prior lessons allows students to associate what you are teaching to broader concepts as part of the larger world view.

Are you an early adopter of the latest electronic gadgets, clothing trends, or whatever is 'shiny and new'? Many school systems can be. They look for whatever program claims to be a researched-based approach to success for their students. I am not here to judge decisions made by my district nor any other district, but to simply warn you to be vigilant of the impact those 'shiny and new' changes might have on your ability to fulfill the duties as an educator. At the end of the day your task is going to be to educate children to the best of your ability by delivering the approved curriculum, so please do be open-minded about new techniques and resources while being mindful that not everything 'new and shiny' is necessarily an improvement on its predecessor.

Having offered you some tips based on my experience to date it is time for me to look ahead. Ever since the first year teaching business studies my time has been spent teaching science. Science is a great subject; I like it but I do not share the same passion for science as I do for the art of business. The change came about after I survived a reduction in force which mandated me to become qualified in additional subject areas, and if you are serious about transitioning into teaching you might consider getting qualified in more than one subject area. My unexpected path included an involuntary transfer to a school which eventually closed, and then a return to my original school building as the science department chair. Three years later I resigned those administrative duties, and I currently teach science in the same department. This year I was honored to be a nominee for Teacher of the Year! What a ride!

My original mission to become a business educator has not changed throughout the course of my career in education. There have been promises made and promises broken for transfer requests back to business education, but the fact is there are few positions available. Also, just like in the private sector, a person can get so proficient at their duties that they get stuck; one science course I teach has achieved a 99% pass rate on state testing! It is my opinion that there comes a time and a place for every educator to consider a change when the zeal and twinkle they had in the beginning is lost. Most new teachers who choose to leave do so in the first five years. To date, I am at the six year mark and again find myself reflecting on my decision to become an educator. I am at that very familiar career crossroad, and I have another tough decision to make. The choice is whether to remain in education or to return to the private sector. I love the teaching and learning process: that look of satisfaction and joy when a student 'gets it' is magical. But in my current capacity as a science instructor, education has proven more political and also extremely more demanding by far of my personal time than the private sector. In education your career path may not be your own to decide because school districts are not as fluid as the private market. My hope is a business position becomes available for me to take on during the upcoming year. So, my final piece of advice is to always have an exit plan. Life is too short.

CHAPTER EIGHT
My Second Big Adventure
by Beth Lambert

Ms. Lambert entered the Career Switcher program in 2010 and she is currently teaching earth science at Granby High School in Norfolk.

MY NAME IS BETH L. Lambert and I can proudly say that I am a teacher, I am changing lives almost every day, and I am impacting the future of my students and of our country. It gives me a tingle every time I say or think this as I know that it is the truth and that I am making a difference. How I got to this point in my life is a rather twisting path and I welcome the opportunity to share it with you.

I was raised in North Fort Myers, Florida with my mother, father, 28 month older brother and my twin brother. We were a lower middle class family with my mother working as a high school English teacher, and my dad was a retired Marine and an elections office official. My mother was a teacher at North Fort Myers High school which my brothers and I all attended. My older brother, Bradly Branson earned a scholarship to SMU University in Dallas, Texas playing basketball, and two years in 1978 later my twin brother and I graduated from high school. My parents could not afford to send us off to college although they did offer to try and assist financially if we continued to live at home and attend the local community college. My twin and I both decided to join the military to get the college financial aid package the services provided at the end of one enlistment. My twin brother Brian joined the Army while I joined the Navy.

I reported to boot camp in Orlando Florida in July of 1978 for what I thought would be a four year period of my life to earn the money for college; it turned into a 30-year adventure sailing the seven seas and touring the world. My military career did not start out very exciting as I wanted to travel to exotic places and see the world and I only had four years of service to get it done. Unfortunately, my first duty assignment was to an aviation training command in Meridan, Mississippi - I didn't even make it north of the Mason-Dixon line! The air station was small and way out in the country about three hours south of Jackson, there was not a great deal to do anywhere close to the base and that's where I spent my entire first enlistment. As with many young sailors, adjusting to the routines and regulations of military life was not without challenges and I found myself in trouble from time to time for breaking the rules. I ended up going to Captain's Mast three times in my first two years. For those of you unfamiliar with military jargon, it is like going to misdemeanor court with the Commanding Officer as the judge passing out corrective measures such as restriction to the base, loss of pay or even loss of rank. As I look back at it now, I knew what the rules were, it just took the Navy a while to convince me that they all applied to me!

As I approached the end of my first enlistment I was preparing to ship my personal belongings home and was looking into colleges close to my parent's home when my Chief Petty Officer called me into his office and said "Let's just call the detailer and see what orders he would offer you, it does not mean you have to take them". I called the detailer and he offered me three years of shore duty on the southern coast of Spain. As I had joined the Navy to see the world as well as to receive money for college, I chose to re-enlist in the Navy for another period to see some of our world. This became the true beginning to my military career.

Luckily for the Navy and for me, my youthful indiscretions were now behind me and I quickly advance to First Class Petty Officer by the end of my tour in Spain. I returned to the United States and joined the Carrier Onboard

Delivery Squadron, VRC-40 in Norfolk, Virginia. I worked really hard during my first year in the squadron and was honored to be selected as the squadron's Sailor of the Year. This privilege allowed me to represent the squadron in the Navy's Sailor of the Year program. I spent the next three months working through the various levels of the competition at successively higher levels winning the competition for Naval Aviation squadrons on the Atlantic coast and the competition for Shore Sailor of the Atlantic Fleet. This qualified me to compete for the final competition for Shore Sailor of the Year for the entire Navy. Never before in the history of the Navy had a female sailor ever qualified for the competition, let alone win it. In May of 1986, I was selected as the Shore Sailor of the Year for the United State Navy and was meritoriously promoted to Chief Petty Officer and served the next year as an aide to the Master Chief Petty Officer of the Navy!

After completing this special assignment, I returned to the fleet and accomplished my goal of seeing the world with assignments in Cuba, Crete, Japan, Hawaii and Diego Garcia.. The combat exclusion law changed finally allowing women to serve aboard combat ships and I embarked on the mighty USS Eisenhower with about 100 other female sailors to be the first females ever to serve aboard a Navy carrier.

My tour on the Eisenhower was successful and I was promoted to Master Chief Petty Officer soon after transferring off the ship. After my promotion, I immediately applied and was selected to the Command Master Chief (CMC) program, which prepares a sailor for the most senior enlisted position in every command. The Command Master Chief is responsible to the Commanding Officer for every area of the supervision, training, and good order and discipline of all the enlisted members of the command. I served three successful tours as a Command Master Chief and then once again made naval history by being selected as the first female Command Master Chief to serve on board an aircraft carrier, the USS Theodore Roosevelt, directly supervising and developing a ship's company of over three thousand sailors.

I served in that position for four years, completed two combat deployments, and I did indeed sail the seven seas and I saw the world!

I transferred to an E-2C squadron to prepare myself for retirement and I left the Navy in May of 2008. As with many retiring service members after a (first) lifetime of service, the primary question in my mind was, now what? Due to my accomplishments in the Navy, I had many job offers to work in the military's civilian work force and also from many military contractors. Most of those jobs were to work in a cubicle or office managing aviation or ship programs or personnel programs from a distance, although for a great deal more money than I made in the Navy. However, as I searched my heart, I knew that I would not be happy doing a job that did not involve a great deal of personal interaction and one in which I felt like I was making a difference. As I transitioned out of the Navy, I attended a resettlement assistance program and one of the guest speakers introduced us to the Troops to Teachers program. This is a program developed and introduced by First Lady Barbara Bush and designed to take transitioning military personnel with a college degree through an abbreviated course of instruction to qualify to become teachers. My mother had taught in the classroom for over twenty years before moving into high school administration, and I know that she was always a little sorry that I chose to stay in the Navy instead of getting out and going to college.

I had earned a Bachelor of Science in Liberal Arts while I was on active duty and looked into the two career teacher transition programs in the local Norfolk area. I selected the program at Regent University in Virginia Beach over the other program due to the quality of the professors that teach the program and the over the top support I received from each and every member of the support personnel, from the program director to the clerical staff.

While on terminal leave from the Navy I signed on with the Norfolk Public School system as a substitute teacher. I thought that this was a good idea as it allowed me to see what it was like in many different classrooms and different grade levels prior to making a decision on becoming a teacher. I strongly encourage anyone considering a transition into teaching to follow this course of action. Different personalities are more suited to different grade levels or to teach different subjects. I spent about a month substitute teaching in all grade levels in elementary, middle and high school classrooms. I also made a deliberate effort to select substitute jobs in the various disciplines from math, science, English and history to the arts, PE and technical fields. I quickly learned that I only wanted to teach at the high school level, and I felt most comfortable in the science classrooms.

For entry into the Career Switcher program I had to take a Virginia state literacy test. The test was comprised of three sections, a reading comprehension, grammar, and a written essay. I had to go to Hampton to take the test and I was amazed at the security protocol they observed. During my thirty years in the Navy with a top secret clearance I attended top secret war briefings that were easier to get into than this test! You enter an outer waiting room and sign in and show your test ticket, then you are buzzed into a more secure area with lockers where you are required to lock up all your personal property. After entering the final testing lab you are seated at an individual computer with blinders on both sides to ensure that no one can see your screen and you cannot see anyone else's screen. I was relieved that I passed this test first time as I would not have wanted to go through all that again! I also took and passed the assessment to demonstrate that I knew enough science to teach the subject at the high school level. I strongly encourage anyone who is considering changing careers into education to thoroughly research the available programs. It is not just getting though all the courses but there is a lot of paper work involved, arranging the practicum placements, and finally seeking a teaching position. Choose a program that has a strong support staff to help you through all the necessary hoops, and research whether the program has a strong relationship with local school systems.

Regent's program was focused to serve working adults as it met on Thursday and Friday evenings and all day on Saturday every other weekend. Although we worked hard during those weekends, we had plenty of time between the classes to work on projects and papers. I found every bit of the classroom time was well worth the time and was focused on skills that we could take into the classroom and use immediately. The practicum portion of the program was great for me and I was assigned to a high school just two blocks from my home. The value of the practicum was different for everyone in my transition class, and I realized it very much depended on the willingness and cooperation of the assigned classroom teacher. After being given my assignment, I received contact information for my cooperating teacher. I was very fortunate that I was assigned to a teacher who welcomed my presence in her classroom and was willing to work with me. She agreed to meet me at a local restaurant a week before I started my student teaching so that we could discuss how to conduct the practicum. I had done a great deal of preparation for our meeting with a proposed schedule of instruction for the entire period including lesson plans, power points, labs, and homework. I was really lucky as she was just starting the oceanography unit on my first day and after thirty years in the Navy I know quite a lot about oceans! I took my laptop with me to show her the power points and materials. She not only agreed to use my materials but suggested that I teach it every day with her in the background to assist if needed. Her only feedback was to shorten the power points and review all the vocabulary I used in all the materials to ensure that I was not using too many advanced vocabulary words that might pose a barrier to learning. She asked me to revise the slides and send them to her prior to the start of my practicum. In the military I had attended many public speaking events where I addressed audiences as large as five thousand people, but I am not ashamed to admit that I was very nervous getting up in front of 30 teenagers for the first time!

The big day arrived and I dressed carefully and professionally and arrived at school early with time to sort out all the material and prepared for the three classes I was to teach. I reviewed my plans with the cooperating teacher and received a pep and confidence boosting talk from her. The bell rang and the students started entering the classroom. The teacher introduced me to the class, cautioned them to take it easy on me, and we got started. Although I had to work through some initial nervousness it quickly passed as my enthusiasm for the topic took over and the classes passed quickly; it was over before I knew it. I loved it! I knew I had made the right decision that this was what I wanted to do. The students were cooperative and enthusiastic, although they wouldn't always be, and all the material was covered. My cooperating teacher gave me feedback at the end of each teaching day to assist me in improving my delivery and classroom management. I found the entire experience hugely useful in preparing me for my own classroom. My cooperating teacher gave me a glowing endorsement to take back to the university and copied the principal of the school. I suspect this greatly assisted me in getting hired there next year, so it pays dividends to make the most of opportunities like this!

Unfortunately not all of my classmates had such a wonderful practicum experience. Some were assigned to teachers who seemed to resent their presence in their classroom, or who were unwilling to allow the student teacher to actually teach in their class. Many of my classmates shared that their cooperating teacher only wanted them to sit in the back of the class and observe although they were very willing to answer any questions at the end of the day. I felt sorry for those who did not have the same great experience that I had and at the time I did not understand the attitudes they encountered. However, after teaching now for six years I know the demands on a teacher are great and sufficient time for everything is a rare commodity. At different times of the year many teachers can feel stretched thin and the addition of a yet another assignment is not always welcomed. I have had two student teachers assigned to me since I started teaching and although it was not always convenient and was an additional drain on my time I remembered how much effort my cooperating teacher put in to make it a great experience for me and so I have tried to assist my student teachers as fully as possible.

Before I knew it I approached the end of Phase I of my teacher preparation program and completion was a week away. Our final assignment was a group project which was a challenge to get all group members' different parts incorporated into a quality project. During the last weekend we took our final exam and presented our project. I was almost sorry to see the courses end as I really enjoyed learning about education and the instructors were wonderful, bright, engaging and supportive. But all good things must come to an end and so with a one-year provisional teaching license in my pocket it was time to find a job.

I applied for an Earth Science position and a few days later received a call from the division with an interview appointment at two of the local high schools. These interviews are usually conducted with the principal of the school and the head of the department you are applying to join. It may sound obvious, but ensure you prepare yourself thoroughly for your interview. Learn about the focus of the school and the department you hope to join. Know how your school preformed on the Standards of Learning tests the previous year, especially if you are applying to teach a Standards of Learning subject. Be prepared to answer questions on what skills and contributions you can bring to your teaching team. Often interviewers will inquire if you are willing to take on additional responsibilities in addition to teaching as many teachers are required to sponsor clubs, classes or to coach a team. Be honest but be cautious because the principal wants teachers who are willing to step up beyond the classroom but the first year of teaching can be overwhelming -- don't take on more than you can chew! My response to this question was that I was very interested in helping out where I was needed but my priority in my first year was to ensure my teaching and classroom management skills were developed to the point of ensuring the success of my students. I was notified the next day that both principals had offered me a teaching position and I had the opportunity to choose which one I wanted to accept so I chose to teach at the school just two blocks from my home!

The first year of teaching is the most difficult and that cannot be overstated; if you survive the first year every following year will become easier. If you are reading my chapter because you are interested in becoming a teacher I am including some points that you might find helpful. After the first year, the lesson plans are in place and only need updating, labs are planned and classroom management skills are honed. After that first year, you only need to work on improving all of the things listed above but during the first year you have to develop all of these things primarily by yourself. In addition to writing a lesson plan for each lesson, planning and acquiring all the materials for the lab or activities, developing the instructional material such as a lecture, power point or computer quest, you will need to plan on how to assess student learning throughout the instruction. You cannot wait until the end of the lesson to assess if the students are getting it because that will be too late. I have found that delivering content in small chunks with a quick activity after each segment allows you to assess their learning as you proceed through the lesson. In addition to all of this, don't forget that everything that you assign will need to be graded and the grades recorded.

Don't be put off by the above as you will get help. How much help you receive depends on your assigned mentors, department and school policies, and how much support the district provides to first-year teachers. I work for Norfolk Public Schools and they have a great first-year teacher support program with a mentor assigned to every new teacher plus on-going professional training. Take full advantage of these training sessions as they are usually run by very seasoned teachers. I was also assigned a mentor from the university who was a retired veteran teacher and I kept a notebook in my classroom and wrote down questions that came up to ensure that I would not forget to ask the advice of these seasoned experts. You will be assigned an in-school mentor who is usually a senior teacher from your chosen discipline. My in-school mentor was my most valuable resource during my first year. He was the team leader for Earth Science with eight years of teaching under his belt so he was very knowledgeable not only in content but in classroom management. He was very supportive during my first year in providing copies of lesson plans especially during the first couple of months while I was trying to master new skills. Members of the teaching team are more willing to share lesson plans with you if you are a good team member. If they are providing the lesson plan, offer to make the copies for the team or collect and distribute lab or activities materials. This is not as challenging as it may seem as all disciplines follow a curriculum pacing guide provided by the district that outlines what you should be teaching and when it should be taught. Rely on the other teachers in your team but ensure that you are doing everything you can to support them in return.

I thought with my background that classroom management would be a breeze. I spent thirty years getting enlisted sailors to do what they did not want to do but I will be the first one to tell you that sailors are easier than teenagers any day. Classroom management is the hardest and most critical of the skills that you will need to master during this first critical year as if the class is not managed correctly very little learning can take place. The inability to manage a classroom is the number one reason that many first-year teachers do not survive their first year as dealing with difficult classes every day can prove to be extremely stressful. You might choose to conduct some inward searching before deciding to teach asking yourself questions such as what skills would you bring into the class, how strong are you mentally, and what grade level do you think you can handle? The older the children are the less likely they are going to do exactly what you tell them, so if you don't have a strong personality the lower grades might be better for you.

No matter where you teach classroom management is a critical skill but where you choose to end up teaching could determine how critical it is. Classroom management in an independent school may not be as challenging as it might be in an urban middle or high school, although every school has behavioral challenges of some type. I teach in an urban high school with a population of over 70% of the students coming from low income families. Many of these children come into the classroom with behavioral challenges that are created by issues in their homes and communities. These are very street-smart children who pick up very quickly if you mean what you say and intend to enforce the classroom rules fairly and consistently. Do not enter the classroom looking for friends, you are their teacher and you need to be respectful and determined in order to maintain a well-managed classroom in which everyone can learn. I have found it pays to start out with firm classroom procedures and rules and be willing to refer misbehaving students to the administration consistently during the first month. This makes for a tough first month but a smoother remainder of the year. Students will realize quickly that you mean what you say and within a few weeks will comply more readily. It is always easier to relax classroom rules later in the school year as you and the students get to know each other better but you will find it almost impossible to firm up or enforce rules if you didn't in the beginning of the year as the students will resent the change. Firm, fair and consistent classroom management from the very first day is what I have found succeeds.

Grading assignments can become overwhelming and I have to resist leaving it for the weekend. Students need quick feedback to determine if they are mastering the material and you don't want to spend every weekend grading papers. Most schools give teachers planning blocks each day. One is used for team planning where all the teachers teaching the same subject will get together to plan lessons, write common quizzes and tests, or to analyze test results. The other planning block is a personal planning block. Use the most of this time to grade papers, make copies, or to assemble material as this will cut back on time you need to stay after school or take home a lot more work to grade.

I found the first four months of my first year to be the hardest but as each month passed I became more comfortable and better able to present the material and to manage my class. Before I knew it SOL test time was just around the corner and that too can be a stressful time for a first-year teacher. It is almost like a final exam test for you although you don't get to take the test! You can count on the last two weeks before SOL testing to be blocked out for review and the only thing you can do at this point is make the most of each class period and have faith and instill confidence in your students. I was very pleased that my SOL pass rate at the end of my first year was 81%. This may not seem very high but I taught six classes of Earth Science and three of them were co-taught special education classes, so this pass rate was a great success.

My first year ended on a tremendous high as I was given the award of being the outstanding new teacher of the year for Norfolk Public Schools. As much as that recognition was wonderful let me share something that made me feel even better. I had a young man in one of my co-taught special education classes who we will call Sam. He had some significant challenges to learning but tried really hard all year long and he stayed after school with me many times as he struggled to master the content. He was not a good taker of tests and he struggled all year long on quizzes and end of unit tests. The morning of the SOL test I brought donuts and juice to school and told all my students that they could stop by my room before first bell to have breakfast. Sam came and got a donut and juice and just hung out in the room. As the first bell rang, I told the students to report to the testing location, I wished them luck, and told them that I believed in them.

All the students left the room except Sam. I told Sam that he need to go and he told me he was too scared. I asked what he was scared of and he responded, "I don't want to let you down Mrs. Lambert". I gave him a hug and reminded him that it wasn't about me but all about him and I knew that if he took his time and did his best he was going to pass. He went off to testing, and by lunchtime I knew that the administrator would know the test results. I went to the Main Office and said I knew that they were not supposed to release the scores yet but I only wanted to know about Sam's result. The administrator looked it up and told me I couldn't be given me the score but did tell me that he had passed. I was so thrilled for him, I looked up his schedule and went to the class he was currently in. I asked his teacher if I could speak to him in the hall for a moment and when he stepped out, I gave him a hug and congratulated him on passing his SOL test. As I stepped back looking up at this sixteen year old, six-foot African American young man, I saw tears streaming down his face. I asked why he was crying when he had passed. He grabbed me for another hug and said "I have never passed an SOL test before!" I told him that he could never say that again as he had now passed mine. I reminded him that if he passed mine he could pass his others SOLs too. Sam passed two out of three tests that year and subsequently he came and said hello to me nearly every day even though I only taught him in ninth grade. I think I was clapping louder than his family when I watched him graduate last year and that is why it is worth getting through that first tough year because few other jobs allow you to have moments like that.

The first year is a learning process. I relied on mentors and seasoned teachers for guidance and advice. Don't be afraid to seek out assistance early when faced with a problem you don't know how to approach. Most teachers are more than willing to lend a hand, share their resources, or guide you to someone that has experience to assist you. Share your concerns with your team mates, your department head and the administrator assigned to your discipline. Their job is to assist you to be successful and they will genuinely want to help you enable your students to succeed.

The final step in that first school year will be your evaluation as a teacher. I found this to be a bit of a letdown due to the fact that I really didn't have a firm understanding of how the system worked. I worked hard all year, had good SOL results and won the new teacher of the year award for the whole school system and anticipated getting the highest marks. This is not how it works and to get the very highest marks requires much more than being good in your classroom. You also have to present at a state or national education convention or to have an article published in an education paper or journal. Once I shared my evaluation with more seasoned teachers they assured me that it was a good one and explained to me how the system worked. My hope is that if you the reader decide to enter the teaching profession that your first year is a great one and that you work through any challenges you encounter. As successful as my first year was it was not without a great deal of stress so remember to take care of yourself and ensure that you do what is best for you to in order to lessen stress!

I am currently in my sixth year of teaching and still teaching ninth grade Earth Science classes. As I wrote earlier, every year after the first year was a little easier than the year before. I am privileged to work with a great team of teachers who work collaboratively to make our delivery of the content better each year. There is often frustration and challenges to overcome. For example the downswing in the country's economy has impacted some public school systems and each year I have taught the amount of money available to buy supplies and materials for the classroom has been reduced. This has an impact on the number of options you have available in your classroom so you just have to use your initiative and do the best you can. I found last year that I had to do more demonstrations in the classroom and less labs as the school did not have the money to buy all the necessary materials.

I entered the teaching profession much later in life than most teachers and I don't have any intention to go back to school to get an advanced degree in an attempt to move into administration. Even if I was younger I doubt that I would want to do so. After six years I find that I still love to be in the classroom sharing the passion for my subject with my students. Every day as I stand outside my classroom to welcome current students to the class, my former students stop by for a word, a fist bump, or a hug. This is a huge part of the joy of our profession. The continual feedback from students that you are an important part of their life and that they know that they are important to you. As I pondered what do to with the rest of my life when I retired from the Navy, I knew I wanted a job that made me feel valuable and one in which I felt I was making a difference. I know in my heart that as a teacher I do that every day

CHAPTER NINE

I am a Pastor
by Chris Martinez

Mr. Martinez entered the Career Switcher program in 2009 and he is currently an Assistant Principal at Poplar Bluff High School in Poplar Bluff, MO.

BEFORE I STARTED TEACHING, I was a pastor, and I still am a pastor. The only change has been now I earn my money by educating young people instead of working in a church. Actually, I was a business pastor. I have a degree in business management plus previous experience in administrating businesses and I also have theological training. Consequently, being a business pastor was relatively easy, but it wasn't fulfilling. I was the 'pastor of paperwork'. Instead of saving souls from the fires of hell and preparing for them for a life in eternity, I saved papers in preparation for future audits. I went to church because I was paid to go to church. That's not a good feeling. Before I was a pastor, I had worked in a doctor's office. That was a good job, but I answered the call to ministry and became a full-time minister.

Before long, however, I needed to find another job, and because my wife was pregnant with our second child I needed a new job quickly. I looked for a job that I could do, but one for which few other people were qualified and so I decided to teach middle school math. For me, teaching is teaching and God has gifted me to teach. I've always been good at it. I knew I was a good teacher because I'm a good learner, and I've helped my friends pass classes when they were having challenges. I always wound up leading our study groups, and I was fairly successful being a youth pastor. I could maintain the interest of students and was able to explain deeper theological truths in ways that made them relevant and interesting.

I learned much in my Master's classes at Regent University that made me a better teacher. I learned the science behind the art of teaching. I learned why some things I did worked and how to make them better, and I learned how ineffective some of the other things were that I was doing. I quickly realized how ineffective lecturing is compared to using other teaching strategies. This was hard for me to swallow because I am a preacher, I love speaking in front of people, I am pretty good at it, and congregations tend to listen obediently! I realized that even though lecturing was enjoyable for me, it was not the most effective way to deliver the curriculum to children. I learned ways to teach subject material in smaller chunks around which I could build activities that engage students in the content. After I had completed the Career Switcher courses I quickly found an opening in Hampton and began teaching math to 7th graders.

I still don't know why they hired me. Maybe they hired me because I wore a tie to the interview but I was just pleased I was hired. They put me on an inclusion team even though in those days I was not sure what was meant by inclusion! The inclusion team comprised the 7th grade special education students. I taught with a co-teacher plus an aide. My co-teacher didn't actually do much. She didn't like math and had a lot of paperwork to do. When she wasn't doing paperwork, she sat in the back and played with her iPhone. The aide on my team, however, was awesome. She knew what worked well and she shared it with me freely. She showed me how to engage kinesthetic learners. We taught graphing liner equations on our feet. She taught me how to be gentle yet firm with students with behavioral problems. She taught me how to pace my class. My class was built around 8-12 minute chunks of activity. It was so fast paced that the students had little time to engage in off-task behavior, and also it left me exhausted. She taught me how to make learning fun, but effective. She showed me the importance of over planning and teaching bell to bell because if I wasn't keeping the children active, they were sure to be way off task. I asked questions and picked her brain all the time. Some of the other math teachers helped me a lot too by sharing strategies that they had found successful. These ladies were truly amazing. They shared their materials and the little tricks they'd found successful over the years. I started singing the multiplication rules even though I am not a singer. If you ever heard me sing, you'd remember it forever because it is so terrible. I'm sure those students on their bad days can still hear my awful song about multiplication rules.

I had the lowest-achieving students. I had students with mental, emotional, and behavioral issues and I had to teach them the hardest subject. One student was pulled out of my class in handcuffs by local law enforcement for the crimes he allegedly committed the night before. In my class he never committed a crime and he did do his work. I liked him, and I think he liked me – it was so sad to see him being led away. I had another student we will call Matthew. Mathew had more energy than ten suns and could get off task faster than any student I have ever met. His parents refused to get him any medication, and they expected me to fix his behavior in my class. In their minds he was off task because I needed to do things differently. So, we learned to do things differently! I changed my pacing, I varied my tone, and I held him accountable. Eventually he and I figured it out together; I learned to keep class moving and he learned to move in the right direction. Another student who we will call Darren was a large 7th grader who really belonged in another class. A substitute teacher was having difficulties as I walked by during my prep period, so I tried to lend a hand. Darren got very loud with me and started charging in my direction. I told him that he was making things harder on himself than they needed to be. He screamed that, "things can't get any harder." I stood my ground and said, "I'm sorry things are so hard on you. I am not trying to make them worse." I think it was a Holy Spirit moment because he stopped dead in his tracks and started crying. We went out in the hall as strangers, and came back as friends. Darren has recently graduated high school. He's now got a job, his own apartment, and a big smile. I had one class of 28 students in the class in which 21 had to have preferential seating. Every seat in my class was preferred. I prayed often. I worked hard. I was a survivor.

I learned how to assess students regularly through different activities. I used white boards and was able circulate around intentionally during guided practice. I learned how to get students involved in learning by designing activities that got them moving and working together. I learned to get them to work hard in class by holding them accountable with a warm and industrious tone. I learned how to get students engaged in math by challenging them and by setting high standards. My class was full of math, but it was fun. We did math on our papers. We did math on our calculators. We did math in our heads, and we did math on the walls. If you can get a 7th grade special education student to work hard and do well in math, you can do almost anything. I learned how to get kids moving and working. I had them perform certain movements for each math rule, and each movement was associated with a different property. When we spoke about the property or used it in class we did the movements. It helped that some of the movements looked like things ninjas might do – they loved that! I worked them from bell to bell. We changed activities often and never let things get boring. Math can be boring enough on its own - it doesn't need our help. I learned how to hold students accountable for their work and involve their parents. I learned how to affirm students and lift the spirits of those students who weren't very good at math. I gave them feedback on their work. I acknowledged the parts of the process they'd get right. I would tell them that math can be hard, but that they were capable. We broke up large processes into smaller steps. Students could master the smaller steps, and put them together to complete the larger process. When students did well I'd call their parents and let them know how proud I was of them. One young girl we will call Nicky was terrible at math. She was good at so many other things, but she could not remember to multiply before adding to save her life. I spend many mornings working with her one on one. Her confidence was broken. Little by little we built on previous successes and she finally passed the class. She didn't get an A, but grade C was a tremendous accomplishment for her. Many students hate math because they've never been good at it. Affirmations go a long way in math.

7th grade math is a tested area in Virginia. We gave common assessments every few weeks and had our results posted in our bulletin. The teachers were ranked against each other and I never wanted to be last. I was never last because I listened to my aide and to the other teachers in my subject area. I loved the kids, and wanted them to do well. It was a difficult year. I was in a new school and teaching new content. I had never taught special education and probably wasn't the most well prepared to do that. My biggest challenge was that I had to learn as much as I was teaching. I had to learn about my students and the best ways to teach my content. I had to be willing to change, quick to ask questions, and brave enough to try new things. I needed more money so I became a bus monitor. That was another experience. I'd ride the bus and ask to get dropped off in the middle of one of the poorer neighborhoods and wait there until someone came to collect me. It was exciting, and it was a little scary. I learned that these kids had difficult lives. They didn't have the home support that others do. They had problems in their lives that were bigger and more dangerous than math problems.

I felt the call to move to Missouri because I had a friend there who needed help with his new church. I applied at the public school there and got a job teaching physics which I taught for a year or two before going back to math. Eventually, I became the teacher of the year in my school. All I did was do the same things I learned in my Master's classes combined with the little tricks my aide had taught me. Once again, I had the kids moving and singing. I had them working together and I chunked my classes to make them seem more fast-paced. Math is a tested area in Missouri too. They don't publish teachers' scores, but I will share with you that mine were the best. There were many differences in the ways Virginia and Missouri approached testing. In VA, the whole school worked together to improve scores in each area. At times, I taught some history, and the history teacher taught some algebra. In MO, people were stuck in their silos. At least, until I got there. I worked hard to build a team among my other math teachers. Now, we work together to tackle the tests.

I succeed at teaching because of the Lord's grace. When others ask me why my scores are so good, I tell them about the aide I worked with my first year. I don't always tell them about the countless hours I pray to the Lord for wisdom and help, but sometimes I do. God is faithful. I am now an assistant principal. I became an administrator because I now have four children of my own, and I needed some extra money. I work hard and don't get involved in any campus dramas so the staff appear to like me. The downside is I miss the constant interaction with my students. I miss seeing the look of excitement on the face of students when they do achieve what they've never been able to do before. I miss watching kids learn, but now I help teachers do their job better so I still help children succeed in school.

Alongside my principal I am responsible for the education of 1432 students. I speak to their parents, and I even visit some at their houses. This summer, two kids ran away and I drove the train tracks to find them. I evaluate 80 teachers. I help them improve their teaching. I pastor them. It's a big and responsible job. I just hope I can do as good a job as my teacher's aide did when I first started teaching in Virginia.

CHAPTER TEN

Teaching Children is a Calling
by Pat McCarty

Mr. McCarty joined the Career Switcher program in 2009 and is currently the Head of School at Norfolk Christian Schools in Norfolk and Virginia Beach.

I WOULD HAVE NEVER ANTICIPATED the challenges I would encounter in the process of switching career, making the transition from an accomplished corporate business executive to a classroom teacher. How hard could it be? As I considered my undergraduate and graduate degrees and assessed my diverse business experiences, I fully expected this to be another simple job change. Several times in my career, I had transitioned into different industries, making me confident that I had the requisite knowledge and skills to teach math or science to a bunch of children. I could not have been more mistaken. As I experienced firsthand my complete ineptitude and unpreparedness, I was quickly faced with great doses of humility and fear, while simultaneously developing awe and respect for those who call themselves teachers.

There is an old adage that says, "Those who can, do, and those who can't, teach." As I complete my sixth year in education, I absolutely reject that notion, not only from my own experience but after having witnessed many who have attempted to become teachers after spending time in other professional and business fields. Some have experienced great success; others have been overwhelmed and ultimately abandoned their quest. I believe that the business of teaching is the single most difficult vocation that anyone who seeks to do it well will ever undertake. The dynamics of the teaching profession range from the strategic to the tactical, from lesson planning to curriculum mapping, from standards-based learning to the assessment continuum, from classroom management to peer collaboration. Teaching encompasses every facet of human interaction from adolescent development to styles of learning, from the "how to" of good parental communication to dealing with overwhelmed department heads, from well-meaning yet stressed administrators to the puzzled looks and curious questions of friends and family. There are so many moving parts that an effective teacher must be a multi-tasking professional who is tender yet has thick skin, while being able to maintain the correct pace in order to have the endurance necessary to stand and deliver every day. And quite uniquely, teaching is the only profession where one can experience exhilaration and exhaustion simultaneously!

When I interviewed for my first teaching job, the senior administrator commented that my resume was unlike any that she had ever seen for a teaching position. That was not the first time that I had been told that my professional career did not reflect a typical path. As a West Point graduate, my first five years were in an Army uniform. Afterwards I sought civilian employment by working in the restaurant industry, fast food to be precise. I managed a restaurant and was soon promoted to an area supervisor overseeing multiple facilities. Three years later I transitioned into the world of medical sales, calling on hospitals in a multi-state territory and completing an MBA, followed by high-tech sales to orthopedic specialists and neurosurgeons. From there, I entered the publishing industry, responsible for warehouses and sales in multiple cities in the western half of the nation and then moved into financial services, ultimately becoming president of a retail operation. My extensive experience of transitioning into new industries and environments gave me confidence that this was going to simply be another new adventure. It was only after I was hired to teach just nine weeks into the preparation program, did I discover how mistaken I was.

My wife actually made the transition first, over my vehement protests and utter amazement. Our youngest son had become very ill so she was not working and was at home caring for him. Once he was well enough to go back to school, she began to do some substitute teaching which got her out of the house and coordinated well with his school schedule. With encouragement from others to consider becoming a full-time teacher, she began to take some classes and I began to get worried that she was serious about it! A seasoned business professional with an MBA does not just step into a classroom of kids and teach. My words to her, almost verbatim were, "Let me get this straight. You're telling me that you want to spend your day with other people's children in a classroom and make little money. Why would you do that?" Not only was I not supportive, I was incredulous. From my corporate mindset, this simply did not make sense. Nevertheless, despite my objections and with only mild support from me, she followed her heart and did just that, becoming a long-term substitute which led to a full-time job as a sixth grade science teacher. I assumed that it would be only a matter of time before she came to her senses. I watched her spend untold hours developing lesson plans, grading papers, researching and studying in preparation for class, talking with parents, attending after-hours school events, and so many extra things that were necessary outside of the workday in the classroom. I had no idea how hard teachers worked at night, on weekends, over holidays and yes, even in the summer when everyone else thinks they are 'off'. Five years later, after watching her and listening to her describe the challenges and joys of teaching, I realized that my high salary did not compensate me for those missing components in my job. I decided that I wanted what she had. So, I left my job, and the majority of our household income, and enrolled in Career Switcher courses designed to enable me become a teacher. I was fortunate (not yet having my teaching license) to be hired by an independent school just a month and a half into my classes and thus entered the classroom with great fear and trepidation as a high school math and science teacher. To this day I am still the junior educator in our household.

As I first stood before that classroom full of ninth and tenth graders, I just knew that there was only one thing they were going to learn that day - that I was not a teacher. I was afraid and so very certain that they would expose my complete inexperience and reveal me as the imposter that I was. But I gathered up my nerve, wrapped in the few weeks of teaching classes I had taken, and used years of business situations and relational tactics to take control of the classroom and make it through that first lesson. I used a great deal of energy keeping them engaged and busy, as I tried to impart that which my well-prepared lesson plan (thanks to my wife's help) had laid out for the day's material. By the end of that class, I felt a complete sense of joy that I had just taught my first official class! The joy was temporary. I quickly realized that the greater challenge of the day was that I had roughly 180 seconds to gather my thoughts, reset and reload, before I needed to do it all over again with a room full of new faces. And then I had to do it again. By the time the school day ended, I was exhausted. But by then, I needed to grade a stack of worksheets the students had done in class and prepare my lessons for the following day. And when that next day came, I would have to review the homework I has assigned them. "Oh my word," I thought, "What have I gotten myself into?" I almost cried.

That first year was a blur. I was still taking my Career Switcher classes while preparing and teaching two different subjects. Several years later, I revealed to those very same first-year students that on a good day I was about six hours ahead of them. They appreciated my candor. I shared that I would be preparing until midnight the material I would teach them the next morning. I would assign them homework, and then go home and do it myself so that I could review and grade theirs. It was an amazing year, although I never felt I could breathe. My second year was so much better, even though I tackled a new subject that replaced one I had taught the previous year. I began to find my rhythm as a teaching professional. I talked with and asked lots of questions of my peers and my wife. I read professional journals from organizations I had joined. I consumed online articles and read teacher blogs. I completed all my Career Switcher courses and continued studies to earn a Master of Education degree. I was becoming a professional educator and I was experiencing the same joy and satisfaction that my wife had tried to explain to me. I was not making any money for a company or making its owners any richer. Far more importantly, I was making a difference.

The amazing complexities of becoming an effective teacher and achieving long-term success can be boiled down to three things: relationships, management, and professional competence. I quickly learned that my students do not care about my resume, or my business experience, or my degrees, or even how I am feeling that day. They needed to know that I cared about them and that I was invested in building relationships with them. I am not convinced that this relational distinctive can be taught. I believe that those who are called to teach likely already have a common desire to make a difference in the lives of their students. If they can effectively communicate their concern and interest in the classroom, they will find that the students will reciprocate in kind. My credibility as a teacher is directly tied to my character, genuineness and compassion much more than to my credentials or content. Relationship-building goes far beyond simply ensuring success in the classroom. As a teacher, I have discovered that caring for and caring about each of my students is a fundamental ingredient in helping me navigate the long and difficult days that are routine in the teaching profession.

One of the most common reasons that some teachers are ineffective, and the one that ultimately leads to their departure from the profession, is classroom management. Getting to know, listen to, understand and relate to children are key components in helping a teacher satisfy the majority of classroom management challenges. Teachers who are good classroom managers are able to maximize student engagement time and seek to create and maintain an environment that allows every student the opportunity to learn. As a teacher, that is my responsibility. No matter the grade, a classroom full of students presents a wildly varied mix of behaviors which can be difficult to corral. Finding the right balance between being too strict and too laid back is a delicate thing, but I treated the classroom like my own home - my students knew my rules and I expected them to understand and follow them. After a couple of students tested me - and they always do - and learned that I said what I meant and meant what I said, it was generally smooth sailing. I also took comfort in hearing of occasional classroom management failures from teachers with decades of experience and so I was encouraged to know that it was not only new teachers who face those challenges. As a Career Switcher I found that being more mature (and maybe a little more intimidating) than most new, freshly-minted teachers helped. I also had lived through the teenage years of my own children which was an advantage and an immense help in understanding what to expect at different age levels.

Professional competence is knowing your subject, being prepared for every class, staying current as a professional educator, and understanding pacing so that the teacher has the endurance to run the entire school year. I made it my modus operandi that I would be fully prepared at the start of every class, regardless of the interruptions this might make to my private life. Lesson plans were ready; homework was graded; worksheets and handouts were copied; technology was warmed up; videos or PowerPoints were loaded, and every other logistical need for the lesson was ready to rock. I also knew that I was responsible to be just as prepared and effective in the first class of the morning as I was during the last class of the day. I owed that to my students. I continually sought to understand the diversity of my students in each class, appreciate their backgrounds and family lives, and adapt for their varied learning needs to increase their opportunity for academic success. I also had to be equipped to teach this generation of students so I could not simply repeat the same rote teaching methodologies that were common when I was a child. The advent of technology and its effective use in the classroom is a challenge to many older teachers. After all, we are digital immigrants and our students are digital natives; they just understand technology intuitively. Kids today are so very different than my generation was at the same age and so I studied and learned to explore and adopted new educational strategies in my lessons.

In business, I tended to devote much of my waking hours thinking strategically; looking down the road one year, five years and ten years out. Although all teachers need to plan ahead, and I do not believe there is a more dynamic environment than that of education, I have learned that it is often best for teachers to live in the moment. Even the best teachers can lose their enthusiasm if they begin to focus on things that are too far down the road. The idea of taking it a day at a time is counterintuitive for me, but my experience in the classroom has confirmed that it is an absolute necessity in order to survive. I do not believe that "inch by inch it's a cinch", but I know, experientially, that "mile by mile it's a trial."

Career Switchers have the advantage of being able to draw on real life experiences in order to provide a big picture view for students. The ability to help children learn how to be critical thinkers, problem solvers and collaborative learners and drawing on application to real world situations is a significant advantage. Conversely, entering an environment with children can be a major frustration as most Career Switchers come from a vocational atmosphere of working with adults who do what they are told and have very different motivations. There is a certain degree of culture shock that comes from entering a classroom full of children who are not and cannot be motivated using the tried and true techniques that work in business. When I spoke in a business meeting, everybody listened. Please know this is not always the case in a classroom!

Teaching, for me, is the most difficult job that I have ever had. This perceived difficulty stems from my own personal expectation that every day in every class I must be a master teacher. My personal goal is to meet the expectation of every student by never missing teachable moments, by engaging them in every lesson, by completing my entire lesson plan, and by assessing what they have learned and re-engaging with the material when I missed the mark. I fully realize that there is a heavy burden placed upon the teacher's shoulders by their students and parents, their peers, and their administration. Often this burden is increased by the teacher's creation of a personal and worthwhile, but unreachable, objective. I believe it is a good thing to not be satisfied as a teacher, yet it is just as important to recognize that nobody gets it right all the time. I never hit a homerun in the classroom. Occasionally, I might have hit for extra bases but most lessons were singles at best and often they were a bunt down the third base line that I barely beat out to first. Sometimes I was even thrown out. But I believe that I never struck out as I entered every class prepared to teach the material and ensure that my students had the environment and the opportunity to be learning. It is not about teaching; it is about learning. It is not difficult to teach all day but if nobody is learning anything it is counterproductive.

I know that being a teacher is the most gratifying and fulfilling occupation that anyone could pursue, but it has to be as a result of being called to teach. Hundreds and even thousands of lives are touched routinely by a single teacher and so there is great reward in pouring ourselves into the young people who sit in our classroom, even if only for a season. Sparking their imaginations, creating passion and enthusiasm for the process of learning, and laughing and learning together is a remarkable gift that is only understood by someone who has made the commitment and sacrifices to do his or her best every day.

I am no longer a teacher in the classroom. Yes, despite my love for students and the relationships that can only be forged over a year together in classes, the headmaster at my independent school announced her retirement and I was encouraged to throw my hat into the ring. Interestingly, as soon as I started teaching, my wife predicted that I would become an administrator. I told her unequivocally, "absolutely not". I love teaching and, having spent plenty of years managing something, my desire, my goal, my mission, was to remain in the classroom. The school board announced they were conducting a national search and, since I am not a lifetime educator, I assumed that any likelihood of obtaining the senior leadership role in the organization was nonexistent. So, I applied for the position of headmaster with little expectation that it would go anywhere.

Last spring, as the headmaster, I handed high school diplomas to the graduates who sat in my first classes when they were eighth graders. I cannot describe the immense joy and satisfaction that came from knowing that, as they left their high school behind to venture into various colleges and careers, I was a small part of their journey. For the first time as an educator, I really began to understand that the greatest reward of teaching is neither the size of a title nor the paycheck, but the greater investment of ourselves into the lives of children who are our own captive audience. When we use our students' time in our classroom wisely the rewards and satisfaction trump anything the business world can offer. I discovered that, despite my preference for being in the classroom, my previous experiences had prepared me to take the mantel of leadership for a school. I miss the classroom so much I ache, but I also realize that I must not be so selfish as to do what I want to do but must be willing to do that for which I have been prepared. Many of my faculty peers, when hearing that I had applied to be the headmaster asked in all sincerity, "Why would you want to do that?" My reply was simple and honest, "It's easier than teaching."

Do not become a teacher if you are not called to do so. We have all sat in classes taught by teachers who appeared disinterested or disengaged and the world of education does not need any more of them. But if you yearn for the opportunity to invest your experience and your knowledge into the lives of students, do not resist - submit fully and use your successes in previous vocations to propel you to success as a professional educator. The military, food services, medical sales, publishing and finance businesses will continue and I am thankful for those who work in each, but in my humble opinion, there is no greater calling than to invest our time and energies in the next generation. And there is no profession that allows one to do so more completely than that of a teacher. I am happy, proud and content to have taken this road.

CHAPTER ELEVEN

From Russia with Love

by Natalia Popko

Ms. Popko entered the Career Switcher program in 2009 and she is currently teaching math at Bayside Middle School in Virginia Beach.

"WHAT DO YOU WANT to be when you grow up?" my mother asked when I was approaching high school. "I want to work with children, teenagers who are in need of guidance and having a hard time navigating through life. A child psychologist, a teacher", was my response. "That's nice", replied my mother, "but who needs a child psychologist in Russia? You will be jobless or underpaid and unappreciated. Being an accountant or a banker is a much better choice". Parents surely know better, I thought to myself. Besides, the finance profession ran in the family.

Fast forward ten years during which time I had obtained a college degree in finance and had relocated to the United States of America. My arrival in the States was followed by working endless hours in restaurants to earn some money and also to improve my language skills. When I was finally confident enough with my English and with my abilities, I applied for a teller position in one of the financial institutions. I remember feeling extremely nervous during initial testing and through the interview process. I couldn't help but wonder "Why would someone want to hire me when there are so many native English speakers? Why would they want to take a chance on me and my accent?" As it turned out, my accent wasn't an issue and my second language proved to be an asset. Getting out of restaurants and making my parents very proud was a great achievement for me. The new job was challenging and meeting different people every day was fun and exciting. I couldn't have been happier at that time.

Two years later, however, the job was becoming more and more boring and meaningless with each day. The routine job responsibilities had been mastered and I was under constant pressure to increase selling. I knew it was a time to move on. It didn't take long before I interviewed and was offered a position at a local bank as a teller manager. New responsibilities, a new team, and new clients kept me engaged and proud of my line of duties for a while. But it wasn't too long before I couldn't shake off the feeling that I was doing something that didn't really matter and I was reinvested with my childhood desire to work with young people.

My decision to become a teacher was not made lightly; it was a culmination of a process of reflection about what I was currently doing with my life and where I wanted my life to be in the future. I chose to follow a career in education because I couldn't think of any job that was more important. I believe that teachers have the ability to not only change the world, but to make it better - one student at a time.

Many of the great teachers I have had throughout my own schooling have become my role models. Great teachers have skills that I wanted to learn and to follow their example. The best teachers in my life were good at explaining content, patient yet firm with students, they were fair, they set high expectations, they knew how to motivate, and used humor appropriately. They had an excellent grasp of their subject matter. This is the type of teacher that I intended to become. I wanted to create a safe and comfortable environment where children can learn so their self-esteem will be increased. In my opinion, a high self-esteem enables children to strive for and accomplish any goals they set for themselves. As a teacher, I wanted to be someone who doesn't just explain, doesn't just demonstrate. I wanted to inspire by going the extra mile, making my students believe that their hopes and dreams are truly within their reach. I believe that every child can succeed when matched with a wonderful teacher, I believe that the circumstances you're born into shouldn't dictate your chances for future success.

I joined a small local non-profit organization called 'Making Difference', whose focus was to provide an opportunity for children to receive additional help in all subjects free of charge. I met with children of different ages and from different walks of life a couple of times a week to tutor them in math. Helping them learn and see them 'get it' made my heart happy! The first time I was tutoring someone and they asked, "Is it really that easy?" I knew I was making the right career choice because it really wasn't that simple! I experienced a joy in seeing the difference I was making as those children gained new insights, became more interested in a subject, and learned about themselves. It made me feel great knowing that I was molding the future through impacting their understandings. Besides, I just loved those 'aha!'' moments!

My mind was set and I began to research teacher preparation programs. There were many options available from a full-time 4 years undergraduate program to a quick six weeks course in the basics. I visited counselors in multiple colleges and made a lot of phone calls, but none of it seemed to be the right fit for me. I didn't want to start over as a full time student considering I already had a degree, nor did I want to go for a short 'quick fix' course. Besides, none of the programs seemed to fit my working schedule which was my sole source of income. One of the colleges offering the Career Switcher programs was Regent University. However, being a private college, Regent University seemed like an unattainable goal for me for financial reasons. I went out on a limb and inquired about the program. To my surprise, the program was offered for the exact same price as other universities. I learned that the program did not only fit my budget, it suited my work schedule as well. I loved the fact that I could choose to take my courses in an accelerated program, or take them more slowly over the period of a year. I chose the longer timeframe so I would be given a chance to really focus and let everything soak in. This was particularly important for me because at that time I knew very little about American public education and I had a lot to learn. Besides, during the course I would be earning 18 graduate credit hours which I would be able to apply toward a Master's Degree. It was time to visit Regent! During the open house, I met a lot of wonderful people who seemed to be pleasant and genuinely caring. I immediately felt that warm, fuzzy feeling inside me and a sense of wanting to belong that I couldn't ignore.

Attending college in the States was overwhelming at first and scary at times, but the overall experience at Regent was truly wonderful! Each faculty member was very fun to work with and provided relevant and rigorous education geared for diversity, teaching methods and cultural sensitivities that in turn enabled us to flourish in a variety of educational settings to meet the challenges of today's profession. Regent's professors were dedicated, informed, and resourceful in creating a dynamic, learner-centered experience. In the process of preparing us to receive teaching credentials, current educational research and theory as well as practical classroom experience were emphasized. I learned a huge amount about how to teach!

After finishing my preparation courses about five months went by until I received a phone call in the middle of October, and I was offered a position with Norfolk Public Schools to teach middle school math. After doing a little research online, I learned that the school I would be assigned to was a high poverty school. At that point all that meant to me was that I had a lots of opportunity to make a difference, and to turn lives around. I was extremely excited and scared at the same time. I pictured the perfect classroom, perfect students, and a perfect learning environment in my mind and I stepped into the classroom...

My first day was very confused and nerve wracking. As I stood in front of the students, expressing how passionate I was about teaching, introducing myself, and presenting my expectations, all I could think was "What did I get myself into...?" I cried myself to sleep that night. The original classroom teacher for these students had left after four days, they went through 12 substitute teachers, and were, suffice to say, not terribly receptive of a scared looking lady (could they really smell my fear?) with a funny accent. In fact, I learned later, they believed that they had "run off" all of the previous teachers and they had the same plans for me. Determined to establish a positive learning environment, and enforcing strict rules and placing high expectations upon my students, I wasn't ready for the challenge that lay before me. I did try all the fabulous tricks I had in my arsenal that I learned in the preparation program, but nothing seemed to be working. From calling home and assigning detentions to buying food and treats and mentoring I tried everything to engage with them. In fact, I felt like I had been shoved into a classroom with more responsibilities than I knew how to handle. I was supposed to know exactly what to do at every twist and turn, but I didn't. Each day became a trial by fire filled with tears – my personal reality TV survival experience! I couldn't understand how children could be so negative and disrespectful to an adult who was trying nothing but to help them, help them to learn, and help them through the tough times of teenage years. Their classroom offenses were way beyond simply talking during instructions and not completing assignments; cussing, fussing, and screaming was very typical. I couldn't understand how they could be so adverse and unappreciative of the free educational opportunities they were given. Coming from a totally different culture where education is a priority and is appreciated, I couldn't make any sense of it. The problems continued to escalate to the point that my classroom was almost out of control - nothing I did or said seemed to work. My students were not listening; my students were not learning. My dreams and desires were truly becoming a nightmare I couldn't wake up from. Even the school's Dean of Students nor any of the student counselors could make them listen to me. I was breaking down under the stress and pressure.

My students didn't respect me, they didn't seem to care about passing the course, or about their future, or about the other children. I felt like I was in the battle I could not win. I started to doubt myself, thinking I was doing something very wrong since my students were exhibiting such a negative attitude towards me and to education in general. All of my dreams and hopes were shattering before my eyes. But more than anything, I felt like I was failing my students and that there was nothing I could do about it. I knew they were not learning enough math from me, the subject that I love and am passionate about, since classroom discipline was an everyday challenge and had to take priority. It was breaking my heart. Right around December, I was ready to resign and to reconsider my career choice. The burden and responsibilities were greater than I could have ever expected.

One of the best pieces of advices I had been given before taking my first teaching position was to 'love those children', even before meeting them and getting to know them. It got me thinking: I knew I cared deeply about my students and their success, but did they know that? I spent my Christmas break evaluating myself, my students, and their circumstances. I realized that I needed to make my 'love' visible. I created a giant bulletin board, crowned it with an 'I "heart" my students' sign, and filled it with inspirational quotes and eye catching stickers and images. I began snapping pictures of activities we did in the classroom, capturing funny moments, friendship moments, laughter moments, successful moments, etc., and posted them to my bulletin board. I couldn't believe how much difference it actually made. I saw my students coming around. It was a slow process, but things were getting better with each day. Negativity that had filled the air became thinner and thinner. I now could teach more and discipline less. I was on my way to developing strong positive relationships with my students that would allow me to be successful and to do all the great things I had always intended. I knew I wasn't going to reach all of my students, I knew that learning a lot of math didn't really happen that year, but connecting with even a handful, even one or two students and passing on my knowledge seemed like a great victory to me and a reason to celebrate. I now know that nothing other than being there and doing the job, pushing through those challenges, overcoming those obstacles one by one, fighting through frustration, disappointments and tears is the only practical way to learn the skills to teach effectively.

After my first year teaching I realized that the chance to inspire a child is not an opportunity, it's a great challenge. I know now that students don't always go to school eager to learn and to solve mathematical problems, they attend because they have to. Lots of time spent learning is not students' top priority but the teacher's job is to teach them. But regardless, students are always learning, and it just may not be what the teacher is teaching. A teacher must not only know a content area, they must also be prepared to teach other "things" such as character, morals, etc. which in some cases might be what they desperately need.

Although my first year was less than desirable, I stand by my choice to be a teacher, to inspire, and to influence young lives. I know I am on the way to becoming a successful educator because I am now in my fourth year of teaching middle school math, and I am responsible for coordinating the work of all the 8th grade math instructors. It is in a different school than the one in which I started, but children are children, many of the challenges are the same, and my recipe of 'loving' the children so they know I care about them works there equally well.

CHAPTER TWELVE
A Colonel in the Classroom
by Joseph Sexton

Mr. Sexton entered the Career Switcher program in 2012 and he is currently teaching history and science at Atlantic Shores Christian School in Virginia Beach.

"FLAPS SET TWENTY PERCENT...door indicates open...airspeed one hundred twenty five knots...slowdown checklist complete. Five seconds...green light!"

I had been through the airdrop sequence dozens if not hundreds of times, but for my copilot students it was only the first, second, or maybe the sixth time they had ever released anything out of a moving aircraft. The 20 mile approaches into Black Jack and All American Drop Zones had become so familiar I could readily identify landmarks, the water tower at Greenbrier, the highway bridge on Interstate 40, a Y-shaped road intersection, a pond shaped like a mitten, and a pasture where the cows ignored the roar of the engines overhead. Flying at the 'school house' had become second nature to me, but it was an experience very new to many of my students, and that is what made each training session exciting, challenging, and rewarding. Instructing at the C-130 Formal Training Unit, known as the 'school house', represented four of my 25 years in the United States Air Force. It was an experience that I thoroughly enjoyed, and it affirmed my enthusiasm and commitment to training and educating our next generation as a teacher.

The seeds of teaching had been planted years before when I returned from the Middle East and the First Gulf War and visited my cousin's third grade class. Sue's class had written to me and sent me dozens of colorful drawings during my deployment. I fell instantly in love with these twenty or so boys and girls. Their bright eyes, smiles, boundless energy, funny questions, unquenchable desire to know more, and their love for their teacher hooked me instantly. I had been in the Air Force for less than four years, but after my visit to this small rural elementary school in my home state of Michigan I had a good idea what I wanted to do when the day came to hang up the uniform. My desire to teach was also inspired by the fact that I had enjoyed so many great educational experiences of my own. Impressions of my early schooling are so strong that to this day I remember many of my classmates and all of my primary and secondary teachers as far back as kindergarten. In my early formative years, each grade, class, and level presented a new world to be discovered and there was always something fascinating to be learned. Like my cousin's third graders in Nashville Michigan, I always had an insatiable desire to learn more.

The military certainly fed my appetite for learning. I was provided one amazing learning opportunity after another, from officer field training, basic flight school, combat survival training, aircraft commander school, flight instructor school, command and staff college, aviation safety school, and war college. Each training course or college presented a unique set of experiences and challenges that expanded my knowledge, improved my skills and thinking, and increased my zeal for learning. My love of learning and for education prompted me to pursue a graduate degree in education administration at the midpoint of my Air Force career. Most of my classmates during the nearly two years of weekend and evening courses were Department of Defense teachers serving overseas in Germany. I learned a lot from them by listening to their tales of classroom experiences. Despite the stories about over-demanding administrators, uncooperative students, behavior issues, unsupportive parents, poor facilities, and lack of resources, I learned that despite the challenges they enjoyed their work as much as I did mine as a military pilot.

I remained in the USAF for another 17 years after earning my graduate degree in education. I enjoyed wearing the uniform, flying all over the world, and meeting the challenges of each new assignment. My wife enjoyed discovering each new location, making it our home, and building new relationships. Our daughters were accustomed to being Air Force 'brats,' packing up their stuff every couple of years and adapting to new friends, new neighborhoods, new schools, and new churches. Like many military families, we got very used to being a family on the move. After a fascinating year living in the Washington D.C. area where I attended war college, we moved to the Norfolk area where I spent the final three years of my career serving on the staff of the United States Joint Forces Command. Working with the other branches of the military was interesting, but I had reached the point in my career where I was no longer part of the operational Air Force that I had grown to love. Several other factors also weighed in. My daughter was approaching her senior year in high school, we were enjoying living relatively close to my wife's family in North Carolina, and our family was ready for a stability we had never known. So I began to plan my exit from the military and worked toward the goals that I would need to accomplish to realize my second calling: becoming a teacher.

With a bachelor's degree in engineering and a graduate degree in education administration I knew I would need more training before I stepped into the classroom. But how much more? Certainly my prior education and my years of military experience had to be worth something. But I was unsure what value they would have in teaching high school students. My interest was to teach history and the social sciences, but I didn't have a history or a humanities degree, and I wasn't particularly interested in taking several years to get another degree. The Career Switcher program was the perfect match. There were several Career Switcher programs offered by universities in the area. I settled on Regent University after meeting with representatives from the university's Military Affairs office and the College of Education. I was drawn to Regent as it is a Christian university as I hoped to teach at a private Christian school. Both of my daughters were attending a Christian school in Virginia and had previously attended a Christian school during their elementary years. Our girls thrived in a Christian education environment, and I wanted to be a part of providing that experience to others. I was not opposed to teaching in the public school system, but my preference was to teach in a Christian school.

I entered Regent's Career Switcher program knowing that it was exactly what I needed to do to gain some practical teacher preparation training and work toward a Virginia state teacher licensure, but initially it was unclear as to the timing of my retirement from the military. The stability and predictability of my job at Joint Forces Command provided an ideal circumstance to take on the Career Switcher program during after work hours and on the weekends. I knew that balancing the demands of a family, a job, and higher education was going to be a challenge, however, I wanted to in the best possible position to start a new career as soon as I left the military. Eventually a date for retirement was set and I was ready to get started!

For one academic year my evenings and weekends were filled with Career Switcher course work. I attended some classes and others I completed online. I got to know many of my fellow Career Switcher classmates and we encouraged, supported, and propelled one another along. There were a few like myself that were preparing to leave the military, but others were from a wide range of career backgrounds, e.g., a chef, a 911 dispatcher, a child care provider, a bank official, and a musician. All were motivated by their desire to teach, and the majority planned to teach in public middle or high schools. The faculty at Regent challenged us, supported us, and inspired all of us to prepare for a new career in education and to stay the course.

The practicum portion of the Career Switcher program was very rewarding and at the same time challenging to manage during my normal work hours. Thankfully, I had a supervisor who was very supportive and allowed me the time I needed away from my job to attend classrooms in two area schools. I observed tenth grade history classes at a large inner city public school and sixth grade History and Bible at a local independent Christian school. The two schools were only a few miles apart from one another but offered me two very different teacher preparation experiences. Both of my cooperating teachers were experienced faculty and went out of their way to provide me with as much helpful advice and practical classroom experience as our brief time together permitted. Despite my practicum being just over the required 25 hours, I drew heavily on that experience at the outset of my initial year of teaching, as it gave me an excellent point of reference from which to begin.

The job search process was a new experience for me as I had entered the military directly out of college. The information I received while attending the military's transition assistance program helped me to prepare a resume, anticipate what to expect during an interview, and translate my military experience into a language and a narrative that a high school hiring authority could understand. I concentrated my job search within the local area. I was not particularly interested in uprooting my family yet again in order to take a teaching job, as "staying put" had been one of the reasons for leaving the military. My prayers were answered when I was hired during the summer by a Christian school only four miles from our home. My previous commute had been over 20 miles in heavy city traffic. I would be teaching history, economics, geography, and physics. Managing four subjects and three preps a day would be a massive challenge during my first year. In addition, physics came as a surprise as I had applied for an opening as a history teacher! My background in math and science, however, filled an immediate need for the school. I was in no position to refuse.

Teaching groups of 17 or so high school freshmen, sophomore, junior, and senior boys and girls five times a day was an entirely new experience for me. Twenty five years of military experience, a father of two daughters, and teaching children's Sunday School had prepared me less than I imagined for what I encountered in my first year of teaching. Most of my students weren't interested in what branch of service I had been in, what rank I had achieved, how many deployments I had been on, or how many places around the world I had flown to and lived in. What they cared about were their friends, what happened at the last game, the latest postings on social media Instagram, and about making the grade and moving on to the next thing. I quickly discovered that fourteen year olds were a tough crowd and that a Christian school was no exception.

Despite the disinterested reception that I received from some of my students, I knew I had something to offer. I was determined to teach them something. I worked, prepared, and taught day after day until I had nothing left. When Fridays came around I was physically, mentally, and emotionally exhausted. Yet there were moments in the classroom that I thoroughly enjoyed. This was what I had wanted to do for so many years, and now I was doing it. But why was it so difficult? My new customers, these 75 young people and their parents, were very demanding on so many levels, and it motivated me to do more and to give more.

In addition to learning the curriculum for history, economics, and geography, adapting to the school environment, relearning physics after 27 years since college, and attempting to keep up with grading homework, quizzes, and tests, I was also taking the Level II Career Switcher courses. Every moment of my week and weekend was committed. I missed many of my daughters' volleyball games, I stopped teaching Sunday school, I curtailed exercising, and I frequently relied on my dear wife and daughters to help me grade the continuous flow of homework, quizzes, and tests. This new career had become all-consuming. It became clear to me why so many teachers are reported to burn out and why so many leave the profession within the first few years of teaching. I was determined not to become part of that sad statistic.

My fellow teachers helped relieve the many pressures of my first year. My supervisor and mentor teacher was a great encouragement and provided a wealth of practical and proven advice along the way. Having come from a military background some 17 years previously, he helped me gain a long term perspective and assured me that the enormous stress I was experiencing was not in any way unusual. His steady confidence and reassurance convinced me things would get better, and indeed they did. Into my second year of teaching I am now experiencing the truth of his wisdom. Several other teachers also came alongside me during this first year. My classroom next-door neighbor who was nearly 20 years my junior but also a first year teacher became my 'battle-buddy.' We frequently commiserated about our many challenges in the classroom and we celebrated each other's successes. We formed a bond that made each of us better and stronger and built a friendship that has carried into our second year. Also influential was my team teacher for tenth grade social studies. Close to my age, he was also a recent Career Switcher and in his second year of teaching. His accounts of what to expect and what worked and didn't work during his rookie year was hugely beneficial. I also learned a lot about how and what to teach by following his lead.

The administration was also very supportive and I knew they were committed to seeing me succeed. When I was at my wits end due to classroom management problems or being pressured by unhappy parents, my principal worked with me to build up my teaching skills and encouraged me to try some creative approaches. Both my principal and assistant principal provided the cover and backup that I needed when dealing with the demands of persistent and unyielding parents. The support of my administration got me through some difficult times.

Finally, my daughters were a great inspiration to me and helped me view my teaching and my classroom from the perspective of my students. Over dinner we would compare our school day. I would gain insights on what their teachers were doing, what the students were responding to, and what they were not. My oldest daughter's English teacher was also in his first year of teaching and it was interesting to get her 'insider's' account of how Mr. E dealt with many of the same issues that I was facing. We had many discussions about why Mr. W was such a great teacher, and why Mr. A had trouble controlling his classroom. My girls were working very hard to please their teachers and it energized me to think that many of my students were working just as hard in my classes.

One of the difficult questions I faced during my first year and continue to grapple with is: How do I know if my students are learning? Were my hours and hours of lesson preparation, the time in front of the class, the notes, the flash cards, the homework assignments, the labs, the special projects, the quizzes, the tests having the desired effect? Were my students getting what they came to school for, and were my efforts paying off? I experienced a wide range of performance levels from student to student and from class to class. My honors class was performing at a consistent A to high B range. They took notes without my prodding. Homework was accomplished on time. Classroom distractions were at a minimum. They walked in the door ready to learn. I wondered if I was challenging them enough. It was a privilege to teach this group of high performers, and it showed me what was possible. However, in several of my other classes, no matter what I did or how hard I worked, the fact remained that many of my students were failing. There were students who repeatedly failed to turn in homework, ignored the assigned readings, refused to take notes, and who were unprepared for quizzes and tests. To no one's surprise these were also the classes in which I was having significant behavior problems. How could I turn around the lack of effort and poor motivation of these students?

124

One technique that bore some fruit was communicating with their parents. Parents had access to a wealth of information online about their struggling student. The online gradebook told the story of each failed quiz and test, a tardy, a low daily grade, and missing homework. I incorrectly concluded that all this raw data would elicit an urgent response from the parents of my struggling students. But nine times out of ten that was not the case. What got their attention was when I made direct contact, either by phone or face to face. In most instances the parents of my struggling students were very supportive of me as the teacher and were genuinely concerned about their son's or daughter's failing grade. In the days and weeks following a conference with mom or dad I would almost always see some improvement in my student's performance and behavior. For some students a single coordinated effort by teacher and parents was enough to break the failure chain and move them toward improvement. However, for several of my students who initially responded to the extra attention at home and school old habit patterns returned and it was right back into the academic red zone.

Another problem involved assessment. I learned over time and especially during my second year that I had not given an adequate number of assessments, specifically quizzes leading up to each chapter test. As the year progressed and as I became aware of what experienced teachers were doing, I realized that I was not using assessments adequately to reinforce learning, expectations, and procedures. For example, I expected them to take notes, but I never permitted open notes during a quiz. I have since discovered that an occasional open notes quiz gives students an incentive to take notes and to do so more carefully. I also discovered that many of my quizzes often failed to reinforce the material that would eventually be tested. This idea of 'you must know everything' was frustrating my students. They didn't know how to study for the test, so many of them chose not to. Because I gave so few quizzes leading up to a test, I typically would not know how my students were doing until I graded the tests.

With many hard lessons learned during the first year I have approached year two more confident, wiser, and optimistic. I see the evidence that my abilities and my students' learning are getting progressively better. I admit that there are still some days that I feel inadequate for the many demands of teaching and wonder if I have what it takes to stay the course and become a successful life changing teacher. I look around and see very capable teachers that are doing that very thing and this inspires me to keep at it despite the grueling labor or my perceived inadequacies. Switching careers was not an easy thing to do. I suspect that because I had spent a quarter of a century doing something that I enjoyed that making an abrupt career change in my late forties was harder than it would have been a decade or so earlier. I learned that switching careers required a well thought out plan, it took time, it took teamwork, especially on behalf of my family, and it took a tremendous amount of effort, endurance, commitment, and passion. I've learned to love kids even when they don't love me. I've learned that the benefit of teaching is not personal recognition, promotion, money, or even the time off during the summer, but instead the satisfaction that I'm doing something that will help prepare and make a positive difference for the generation that follows.

9 780991 104680